FAMILY PLANNING IN SLUM AREAS

FAMILY PLANNING IN SLUM AREAS

KAMINI JAIN

GYAN

GYAN PUBLISHING HOUSE

NEW DELHI-110 002

ISBN : 81-212-0449-6
Library of Congress Card No. 93-900304

Published in 1993 by
Gyan Publishing House
5 Ansari Road
New Delhi-110002

Composed by Bharadwaj Printo Graphics, New Delhi-110007
and
Printed at Goyal Offset Works, Delhi

CONTENTS

PREFACE

Family planning means limiting the final size of their family by men and women who are directly responsible for the birth of their children. It is not restricted to deciding how many children, and how often, a family want it also means using modern methods of birth control to achieve the desired goal. One important reason for practising birth control is the protection of a woman's health. Many times a woman, who has borne many children in quick succession, is so physically exhausted and enfeebled that she cannot take care of her children properly. If a woman stops having babies after she has borne two or three children, she can spend more time in taking care of their needs. It is very hard for a woman to keep more children neat and clean and to help each one whenever they need her.

There are also some other reasons for practising family planning. Parents can protect their children's health more effectively, if they have a small, well-spaced family. A mother's health will be better if she has two or three children. A family's income goes further if there are a few children in the camily. Parents can give each child a better start in life if they have a small family. Birth control can help our society in becoming stronger and richer.

Problems arising out of an unplanned family are most acute in slum areas, which are inhabited by the economically weaker section of society, many of whom live below the poverty line. A majority of them are utterly illiterate, their means of livelihood being manual labour or working as petty hawkers. Their woman work mostly as unorganised domestic labour.

The slum areas are in unplanned aggllomeration of kaccha dwellings, often insanitary, unhygienic, and ill-ventilated, a veritable breeding ground of disease and ill-health. The idle and the unemployed often deal in illicit liquor and satta, many being themselves addicted to drink, drugs and gambling living as parasites on their women's meagre earnings, often forcing their children of school-going age to earn their keep. In the absence of any means of wholesome recreation, and also because the labour of their children is economically profitable to them, they breed indiscriminately with little or no regard to planned and responsible parenthood.

A study of family planning in slum areas offers plenty of scope for the investigator, particularly when no such full-length study has been undertaken so far on the slums of Hoshangabad, a historical town on the banks of the holy Narmada near Bhopal.

The book has been divided into ten chapters. Chapter I, serving as an introduction, specifies the objectives, research design, methodology, and limitations of the study. Chapter II places family planning in its proper perspective from the pre-independence days to the ost-independence period. Chapter III deals with the slums of urban Hoshangabad and analyses the personal data of the families covered by the sample survey. Chapter IV takes into account the family data of the slum residents and their relevance to birth control. Chapter V examines and interprets the economic data in the context of family planning.

Chapter VI evaluates the extent of family planning consciousness among the slum families surveyed. Chapter VII investigates the family planning methods adopted by the slum families. Chapter VIII discusses the role of incentives in promoting planned parenthood. Chapter IX makes a critical assessment of the opinions and attitudes of slum families on the various aspects of fertility control. Chapter X correlates the discussion of the previous chapters and deduces the conclusion.

I avail myself of this opportunity to place on record my indebtedness and profound thanks—

To my esteemed mentor, Professor I.S. Chauhan, M.A., Ph.D. (ANU, Canberra, Australia). Head, Department of Sociology, Bankatullah University, Bhopal, whose unfailing guidance and opportune advice had been of immense help in the completion of this modest work;

To Shri Vijay Singh, recipient of an award by the President of India and retired administrator, for his kindness in clarifying some points that intrigued me;

To my dear mother Shrimati Devika Rani and my dear father, the late Shri B.L. Naga, retired Assistant Sales Tax Commissioner, who, always cooperative and encouraging, boosted my morale whenever it tended to me;

To my elder brother, Shri Pradeep Naga, who did most of the running about in connextion with the preparation of this study;

To the Librarians, Divisional Library (Hoshangabad), Government Home Science College (Hoshnagabad), Barkatullah University (Bhopal) and Family Planning Association of India (Bhopal) for placing at my service whatever material relevant to the area of study they had on their bookshelves;

To my respondents who were good enough to spare some of their time in receiving me at their homes and answering my queries;

To all my friends and well-wishers who, in one way or the other, shared the burden of tabulation, calculation, proof-reading of the typescript, and related activities. and last, but not the least.

To Miss Aparna Rajurkar for her laborious effort in typing the manuscript.

Government Home Science College,
Hoshangabad, M.P.

(KAMINI JAIN)

LIST OF TABLES

Chapter I

INTRODUCTION

Objectives, Research Design, Methodology, Limitations

Hoshangabad, as its name implies, was founded by Sultan Hoshang Shah Chori in the latter half of the fourteenth century. The Sultan built a strong fort on the bank of the river Narmada, which is now in ruins, to defend his kingdom against invaders, particularly against the Gond Kings of the tracts now in district Betul. He lived, ruled, and died in Hoshangabad. The area subsequently became a part of the dominions of the Sultan of Mandu till 1567, when it passed on to the Mughals.

In the eighteenth century, the territory comprising Hoshangabad and its neighbouring areas was captured by the Gond Kind of Mandla. In 1726, Dost Muhammad Khan, the founder of the erstwhile Bhopal State, taking advantage of the internecine wars among the Gond Kings, invaded Hoshangabad and annexed it to his State. The Bhonsles of Nagpur captured this area and their sovereignty covered the period between 1740 and 1775. Subedar Beni Singh Conquered the Hoshangabad Fort in 1776 and declared himself as the new ruler of Hoshangabad. In 1802, Nawab Wazir Muhammad Khan of Bhopal overpowered the Subedar and advanced towards Sohagpur but, facing strong opposition from its Gond King, retreated. Three years later, in 1805, the Sindhias of Gwalior conquered this area and handed it over to the Bhonsles to administer it on their behalf.

The period between 1805 and 1818 was one of complete breakdown of law and order. Robbery and dacoity were rampant. The Pindaris plundered and ravaged village after village until the British commander, Adams, restored law and order and established British rule in January 1818. A British agent was headquartered in Hoshangabad to supervise the administration. In 1835, the area of the district was extended to include Narsinghpur in the east and Betul in the west. The freedom movement of 1857 did not affect the district, and it remained under British control till 1947.

Certain fossils and ancient monuments reveal that the area was populated in ancient times also. Stone implements discovered by the Archaeological Department date back to the prehistoric era. Fossils, idols, and axes were discovered at a site near the confluence of the river Tawa and the river Narmada, substantiating the theory that patches of human civilisation developed on the river banks. The *Narmada Puran* was written during the mythological period. Narmadapur in Hoshangabad is an ancient holy place on the bank of the river.

Both the Shankaracharya, who founded the Sanatan Dharma, and Ramanuj passed much of their life-time in the Narmada valley in meditation and prayer. The South Indians seem to hold the Narmada in greater veneration than the Ganga, and flock to

Hoshangabad in their thousands every year for a holy dip in the river. Several annual fairs are held in different places in the district, among which the Bandrubhan fair is the most important.

No documentary evidence is available regarding this area in the ancient times, but some scholars connect it with the period of the Mahabharat. However, stone inscriptions prove that the area was under the domination of the Parmar dynasty of district Dhar for about three hundred years from the ninth century to the twelfth century. During the thirteenth century and larger part of the fourteenth century, the Tomars and the Chauhans ruled this territory until Hoshang Shah assumed power.

Present-day district of Hoshangabad

At present, Hoshangabad is an important district of Madhya Pradesh, spread over an area of 7,442.9 square kilometres, and divided into four Tahsils—Harda (2,524.9 sq km), Sohagpur (2,105.5 sq km), Hoshangabad (1,786.2 sq km), and Seoni-Malwa (1,026.3 sq km). The entire district has 13 towns and 1,558 villages. The district headquarters, the Sports Department of Madhya Pradesh, and the divisional headquarters of four departments—revenue, forest, education, post and telegraph—are all located at Hoshangabad. Security paper mill, which makes paper for currency notes, has also been established there. The Tawa Project is the largest irrigation project of Madhya Pradesh. The Agricultural Research Institute at Pawarkheda, affiliated to Jawaharlal Agricultural University, conducts soil analysis and research on wheat. At Budni, 5 miles away from Hoshangabad, training is imparted to cultivators in tractors and maintenance of agricultural implements. Near Babai, a large 9,307-acre modern farm is maintained by the Agro-Industries Corporation of Madhya Pradesh.

The Tawa Multipurpose Project was completed with the assistance of World Bank at a cost of Rs. 63.47 crores, and dam and irrigation experts from West Germany still visit the site periodically for monitoring purposes. The dam over the river Tawa is 29 miles away from Itarsi on the eastern side of Hoshangabad. The height of the dam varies between 57 metres and 91 metres at different places. It is 1,598 metres broad. A total number of 3,082 persons had to vacate the villages which were submerged. The length of the left-bank canal is 183 km, while that of the right-bank canal 159 km. The estimated area of land irrigated by the canals approximates 2,46,869 hectares.

The irrigation facilities have increased not only the production per acre but have also facilitated the introduction of the double cropping pattern. The benefits of the project extend to as far as Tahsil Sohagpur in the east, and to Tahsil Harda and Tahsil Seoni-Malwa in the west. The department of Fisheries expected large-scale production of fish from the dam, but the expectations have yet to be fulfilled. A 100-acre fish farm was constructed near Powarkheda, but it too has failed to produce the desired results. The large expenditure incurred on the development of fishery seems to have gone waste, as the whole fish-production scheme has ended in a fiasco.

Population : Rural and Urban

Table 1 presents comparative data on population distribution on the basis of rural and urban of Hoshangabad according to the Census of 1971 and the Census of 1981.

Table 1

HOSHANGABAD : DISTRIBUTION OF POPULATION RURAL AND URBAN

1971 and 1981

Population	*1971*	*1981*
Total	8,05,870	10,03,939
Rural	6,30,442	7,51,855
Urban	1,75,428	2,52,084
Rural-urban ratio	78 : 22	75 : 25

Source : *Pocket Compendium of Madhya Pradesh Statistics,* Directorate of Economics and Statistics, Bhopal, 1986, p. 10.

The table reveals that, during the decade 1971 and 1981, the population of Hoshangabad, increased by 1,98,066 (from 8,05,870 in 1971 to 10,03,936 in 1981). A similar increase of 1,21,416 rural population is noticeable (from 6,30,442 in 1971 to 7,51,855 in 1981). Urban population also registers a rise of 76,656 persons (from 1,75,428 in 1971 to 2,52,084 in 1981). The rural-urban ratio has also grown in favour of urban population from 78 : 22 to 75 : 25, leading to two major inferences.

First, Hoshangabad remains basically a district with three-fourths of its population being rural-based, and only one-fourths urban-based. Secondly, the slight tilt of the population towards urban areas suggests that the availability of irrigation facilities has reduced the demand for agricultural labour, who have migrated to urban centres in search of employment. The divisional headquarters of the departments of education, forest, revenue, post and telegraph, the Agricultural Research Institute and the Fishery Farm of Powarkheda, the Tractor Organisation at Budni, the Agro-Industries Corporation near Babai, and the Security Paper Mill must have also added to the urban population.

Density of population, sex ratio, decennial growth rate

Table 2 provides data on the density of population, sex ratio, and decennial growth rate according to the Census of 1981.

The table shows that, as compared to neighbouring Bhopal whose density of population is 323 per sq km, Hoshangabad lags far behind : its density being only 100 per sq km. Males out number females by 92 per thousand which is difficult to explain except in terms of death-rate which tends to be greater for females perhaps because females are still a neglected lot in most villages. As compared to the decade 1961-1971, the succeeding decade (1971-1981) witnesses a fall of 5.76 per thousand population mainly owing, among other causes, to the family planning drive.

Table 2

POPULATION DENSITY, SEX RATIO, DECENNIAL GROWTH RATE HOSHANGABAD

1981

Particulars	*Figures*
Density of population (per sq km)	'00
Total population	10,03,939
Male population	5,26,273
Female population	4,77,656
Sex ratio (females per 1,000 males)	908
Decennial growth rate 1961-1971 (per 1,000 population)	30.34
Decennial growth rate 1971-1981 (per 1,000 population)	24.58

Source : *Pocket Compendium of Madhya Pradesh Statistics*, Directorate of Economics and Statistics, Bhopal, 1986, p. 4.

Projected Population

The Directorate of Economics and Statistics, Madhya Pradesh, Bhopal, undertook the exercise of making district-wise annual projections of population from 1981 to 1991. It must have kept in mind the effect of family planning in reducing population growth. Its projections relating to Hoshangabad are delineated in Table 3.

Table 3

HOSHANGABAD : PROJECTED POPULATION

1981-1991 *(Thousand)*

Year	*Population*	*Annual growth*	*Growth since 1981 (i)*
1981	1003	—	—
1982	1023	20	20
1983	1044	21	41
1984	1062	18	59
1985	1087	25	84
1986	1108	21	105
1987	1131	23	128

1988	1153	22	150
1989	1177	24	174
1990	1200	23	197
1991	1224	24	221

Source : *Pocket Compendium of Madhya Pradesh Statistics,* Directorate of Economics and Statistics, Bhopal, 1986, pp. 46 and 49.
(i) Calculated by the writer.

The Directorate of Economics and Statistics have not explained the factors on the basis of which the annual increase of the population of Hoshangabad was calculated. For example, the annual growth per thousand of population is calculated at 23,000 persons for 1987 : it is reduced to 22,000 individuals for 1988; it is increased to 24,000 persons for 1989, again lowered to 23,000 persons for 1990, and again raised to 24,000 persons for 1991, which is the same increase as projected for 1989.

However, what is clear is that the population of Hoshangabad is estimated to rise to approximately 12,24,000 in 1991 from approximately 10,03,000 in 1981, showing an increase of around 2,21,000 persons in 10 years. As compared with Table 1, the increase during 1971 and 1981 was that of 1,98,064 persons.

Annual rainfall and rainy days

As rainfall is essential not only for forest fauna and flora but also for agriculture, the mainstay of the foodgrains and fodder, vegetables and fruits, oilseeds and cash crops production, Table 4 furnishes data on the average rainfall and the number of rainy days for the four-year period between 1979-80 and 1982-83.

The vagaries of the Indian monsoon are proverbial, which are confirmed by the figures of average annual rainfall and the number of rainy days in Hoshangabad delineated in the table. The average rainfall was the highest in 1981-82 (1,366.8) mm, and so were the number of rainy days (62). It was the lowest in 1979-80 (950.9 mm), the rainy days numbering only 38—

Table 4
ANNUAL RAINFALL AND RAINY DAYS HOSHANGABAD
1979-89 to 1982-83 *(Millimetres)*

Year	*Average Rainfall*	*Rainy Days*
1979-80	950.9	38
1980-81	1,222.3	55
1981-82	1,366.8	62
1982-83	1,072.8	50

Source : *Pocket Compendium of Madhya Pradesh Statistics,* Directorate of Economics and Statistics, Bhopal, 1986, p. 53.

presenting almost near drought conditions which affect rainfed agriculture adversely. The average rainfall during the four years, taken together, adds up to 1,53.2 mm, and the number of rainy days to 51.25, which are greater than in many other districts of Madhya Pradesh.

Distribution of fertilisers through cooperative agencies

The fairly good rainfall in district Hoshangabad, together with additional large-scale irrigation facilities available to the farmers of Hoshangabad on account of the Tawa Multipurpose Project has given a boost to agriculture, enabling cultivators to have two crops a year in place of the traditional single crop, and in making use of improved varieties of seeds and, alongwith organic manure, making use of chemical fertilisers (nitrogen, phosphate, and potash). Chemical fertilisers are utilised to best advantage where adequate water is available.

Table 5 projects data on the distribution of chemical fertilisers through cooperative societies to Hoshangabad farmers during the five-year span 1978-79 to 1982-83.

The table points to the modernisation of agriculture by the increasing use of chemical fertilisers. In this connection, the contribution of the Agricultural Research Institute at Powerkheda in educating the farmers and the block development staff cannot be overlooked. The largest quantum of annual increase of chemical

Table 5

HOSHANGABAD : CHEMICAL FERTILISERS DISTRIBUTION THROUGH COOPERATIVE SOCIETIES

1978-79 to 1982-83 *(Million Tonnes)*

Year	*Quantity*	*Annual increase (1)*
1978-79	2,075	—
1979-80	2,400	325
1980-81	2,975	575
1981-82	3,897	922
1982-83	4,475	578

Source : *Pocket Compendium of Madhya Pradesh Statistics,* Directorate of Economics and Statistics, Bhopal, 1986, p. 87.
(1) Calculated by the writer.

fertiliser utilisation (922 million tonnes) in 1981-82 synchronises with the highest amount of rainfall in that year vide Table 4, establishing the close correlation between the use of chemical fertilisers and the adequacy of water availability. The point gains added strength by the fact that in 1981-82 rainfall was higher (1,222.3 mm) and the number of rainy days were more (62) than in the previous year (1980-81), and so the quantity of fertilisers consumed increased by 922 million tonnes. In contrast, in 1982-83, both rainfall (1,072.8 mm) and the number of rainy days (50) declined over the preceding year, and consequently the annual increase in fertiliser consumption also declined to 578 million tonnes.

However, the consumption of fertilisers shows a consistently rising trends year by year. In 1978-79 it stood at 2,075 million tonnes, increasing to 2,400 million tonnes in 1979-80, then rising to 2,975 million tonnes in 1979-80, then rising to 2,975 million tonnes in 1980-81, then escalating to 3,897 million tonnes in 1981-82, and finally shooting up to 4,475 million tonnes in 1982-83. The table deals with fertiliser distribution through cooperative societies, but if we include the purchase of fertilisers by farmers from private retailers, the quantity of fertilisers actually used by Hoshangabad farmers will go still higher up.

Forest area and forest types

Forests attract rainfall and help in maintaining ecological balance, besides being a grazing ground for cattle, serving as the sole source of supply of timber, bamboos, fuelwood, and minor forest produce useful for industrial, commercial, and domestic purposes, and promoting forest-based industries. Madhya Pradesh has an extensive forest cover, equalling 30.09 per cent of its total geographical area. Table 6 puts forth data on the forest area of district Hoshangabad as estimated in 1980-81.

Table 6
HOSHANGABAD FOREST CIRCLE FOREST AREA AND TYPES
1980-81 *(Sq. km)*

Description	*Area*
Total forest	7,372
Reserved forest	4,831
Protected forest	2,534
Percentage of total forest area to geographical area	36.72

Source : *Pocket Compendium of Madhya Pradesh Statistics,* Directorate of Economics and Statistics, Bhopal, 1986, p. 125.

The table reveals that the percentage of total forest area to total geographical area of district Hoshangabad (36.72) is greater by 0.63 per cent as compared to that of Madhya Pradesh (35.09), and that out of the total forest area, more than half is reserved forest, while the rest is protected forest. There is no "unclassed" forest, as there is in many other districts of the State.

Government employees

The number of Government employees in a district is one of the indicators of its progress in civil and police administration, health and educational services, and the projects in force there. Table 7 presents comparative data on the service class-wise distribution of Government employees in district Hoshangabad in 1982 and 1983.

Table 7

HOSHANGABAD : GOVERNMENT EMPLOYEES SERVICE CLASS-WISE

As on 31 March 1982 and 1983

Particulars	*Number*
Total Number of Government employees in 1982	12,772
Percentage of total Government employees to those in Madhya Pradesh	2.35
Total number of Government employees in 1983	13,265
Percentage of total Government employees to those in Madhya Pradesh	2.42
Government employees Class I	77
Government employees Class II	603
Government employees Class III	11,294
Government employees Class IV	1,651

Source : *Pocket Compendium of Madhya Pradesh Statistics,* Directorate of Economics and Statistics, Bhopal, 1986, p., 150.

The table discloses the slight increase of 493 persons in the number of Government employees, from 12,772 in 1982 to 13,265 in 1983, which suggests either expansion of staff in some departments or the introduction of some new minor projects in the district. The percentage increase in Government employees in Hoshangabad between 1982 and 1983 is marginal (0.07 per cent), from 2.5 per cent in 1982 to 2.42 per cent in the succeeding year.

Branches of commercial banks

The number of branches of commercial banks serve as one of the pointers to the socio-economic development of a district, particularly when the branches are located in rural centres. Table 8 gives data on the number of branches of commercial banks in Hoshangabad district in 1981.

According to the table, district Hoshangabad had as many as 66 branches of commercial banks in 1981—the majority of them (37) located in rural centres, compared to 29 in semi-urban centres. During the 9 years that have elapsed since 1981, it is likely that the number of branches of commercial banks

Table 8

HOSHANGABAD : COMMERCIAL BANKS' BRANCHES

As in June 1981

Particulars	*Number*
Rural centres with a population up to 10,000	37
Semi-urban centres with a population of over 10,000 and up to 1,00,000	29
Total	66

Source : *Pocket Compendium of Madhya Pradesh Statistics,* Directorate of Economics and Statistics, Bhopal, 1986, p. 175.

must have increased further due to increased economic and commercial activity in the district, but no authentic statistics are available for these years.

Bank deposits and advances

The amount of deposits in banks and the amount advanced as loans by the banks speak of the saving habits of the people, the commercial transactions through banks, and the loans advanced for developmental purposes and for employment-generating schemes in the district. Table 9 offers data on the deposits in the scheduled commercial banks of district Hoshangabad and the advances made by them.

Table 9

HOSHANGABAD : DEPOSITS AND ADVANCES SCHEDULED COMMERCIAL BANKS

As on 31 December 1982 *(Lakh rupees)*

Particulars	*Amount*
Deposits	3838
Advances	2296
Percentage of advances to total deposits	59.8

Source : *Pocket Compendium of Madhya Pradesh Statistics,* Directorate of Economics and Statistics, Bhopal, 1986, p. 179.

The table discloses that the percentage of advances disbursed by the scheduled commercial banks to total deposits in district Hoshangabad comes to 59.8, which is higher by 1.7 per cent compared to that of Madhya Pradesh as a whole (58.7). The total amount of bank deposits and the amount advanced as loans are also higher than those in the economically and socially and socially backward districts of the State.

Post Offices

The network of post offices in a district indicates the extent of communication facilities which link people with other people. The number of head post offices in a district points to the amount of work-load. Mobile branch offices suggest the availability of postal services to remote and thinly populated villages in a district. Table 10 presents data on the number of post offices functioning in district Hoshangabad during 1982-83.

Table 10
HOSHANGABAD : NUMBER OF POST OFFICES
1982-83

Description	*Number*
Head offices	2
Departmental sub-offices	49
Extra-departmental sub-offices	38
Extra-departmental branch offices	166
Mobile branch offices	173
Total	428

Source : *Pocket Compendium of Madhya Pradesh Statistics,* Directorate of Economics and Statistics, Bhopal, 1986, p. 206.

Literacy

Literacy emancipates men and women from the prison of darkness and ignorance. It enables them to read and write and, if the desire be with them, to get themselves acquainted with new ideas, to become aware of what is happening around them and in the world, to bid goodbye to irrational beliefs, practices, and superstitions, and to adopt a scientific and rational outlook. Table 11 offers comparative data on the percentage of literacy among the male and female population of district Hoshangabad according to the Census of 1971 and the Census of 1981.

Table 11

HOSHANGABAD : PERCENTAGE OF LITERACY MALE AND FEMALE POPULATION

1971 and 1981

Description	*1971*	*1981*	*Decennial increase (1)*
Persons	29.56	35.35	5.79
Male	41.81	47.58	5.77
Female	16.15	21.88	5.73

Source : *Pocket Compendium of Madhya Pradesh Statistics,* Directorate of Economics and Statistics, Bhopal, 1986, p. 281. (1) Calculated by the writer.

The percentage of literacy, according to the table, increased by 5.7 during 10 years, which comes to around 0.58 per cent annual increase, which is hardly encouraging. Literacy among the male population of Hoshangabad is only marginally higher by 0.03 per cent than among the female population during the entire decade. This shows that social welfare organisations, the education department, and the adult literacy programmers must pay greater attention, particularly to the rural female population, to achieve a reasonable degree of literacy in the shortest period possible to uplift society to an educationally respectable level.

School education

School education includes education up to three levels—primary (Class V), middle (Class VIII), and 10 + 2 (Class XII) imparted in private schools, State Government Schools, Central Schools, and the rural Navodaya Schools, some of them being co-educational, Table 12 provides data on the number of schools, the number of students, the number of teachers, and the expenditure incurred on them in district Hoshangabad during 1981-82.

The table shows that for a population of 10,03,939, the number of schools are 1,368, which comes to an average of one school per 733.87 unit of population. The number of students in these schools is 1,56,765, which means an average of 114.59

Table 12

HOSHANGABAD : SCHOOL EDUCATION SCHOOLS, STUDENTS, TEACHERS, EXPENDITURE

1981-82

Description	*Number/Amount*
	Rs.
Schools	1,368
Students	1,56,765
Teachers	4,387
Expenditure	43,504 lakh

Source : *Pocket Compendium of Madhya Pradesh Statistics*, Directorate of Economics and Statistics, Bhopal, 1986, p. 307.

pupils per school. The number of teachers being 4,387, the average teacher : pupil ratio works out to around 1 : 36, which is fairly satisfactory.

Non-agricultural enterprises and their workers

Non-agricultural enterprises are meaningful in that they absorb a part of the rural and urban unemployed population. The more such enterprises, the more the employment they generate. As an alternative to the overwhelming pressure on the Government for the almost impossible task of creating jobs for all the unemployed people, both agriculture-based as well as non-agricultural enterprises, preferably in the private sector, play a socially and economically productive role. Table 13 places data on the number of non-agricultural enterprises in the rural as well as the urban areas in district Hoshangabad, together with the number of persons normally engaged therein.

The table reveals that the total number of non-agricultural enterprises, in rural and urban areas combined together, is 24,318, while the number of persons usually working there is 62,205, which comes to the tiny figure of an average of 2.55 persons per enterprise, suggesting that these enterprises are mini ones.

The number of rural enterprises is 13,292, employing 19,988 persons, which implies the almost neglible figure of an average of 1.50 persons per enterprise. In other words, out of the total rural population of 6,30,442 (Table 1), only a minor proportion of 19,988 persons are employed in rural non-agricultural enterprises.

Table 13

NON-AGRICULTURAL ENTERPRISES AND THEIR WORKERS RURAL AND URBAN HOSHANGABAD

1980

Description	*Number*
Rural non-agricultural enterprises	13,292
Urban non-agricultural enterprises	11,089
Total	24,381
Workers engaged in rural enterprises	19,988
Workers engaged in urban enterprises	42,217
Total	62,205

Source : *Pocket Compendium of Madhya Pradesh Statistics,* Directorate of Economics and Statistics, Bhopal, 1986, p. 402.

The number of urban enterprises are 11,089, employing 42,217 persons, which works out to an average of 38.07 persons per urban enterprise, denoting that urban non-agricultural enterprises are a little larger than the rural ones. Further, in an urban population of 1,75,428 (Table 1), these enterprises provide employment to 42,217 persons, which suggests that there is less unemployment in the urban sector of Hoshangabad than in its rural sector.

Slums

In our country, as in many other countries, there is hardly a city without its eyesores, and Hoshangabad is no exception. Slums are for those families who do not have the means to pay the high rent of a house, not to speak of owning one. Slums are the enforced habitat of families which are economically, socially, and educationally weak. The worst slums comprise of shanties, or make-shift structures of tin sheets, plastic sheets, even old gunny bags, mud or brick walls, without any plan or pattern, and are unauthorised structures on encroaches Government land. Each such shanty, jhuggi or jhonpri measures on an average approximately between 8 and 10 feet in length, and between 6 and 8 feet in breadth, with a roof of tin or plastic sheets at a height varying between 6 and 8 feet. The flooring is entirely of mud. The abode has only a single narrow door and no window. Thus it is often damp and dark, with neither flow of air nor sunlight. All these factors are most conducive to the growth of disease-bearing bacteria.

A small-size jhuggi serves as kitchen, as bedroom, as store-room, and sometimes the small space facing the road as a petty shop. When used as a kitchen, it is filled with smoke, excess of which is harmful not only for the eyes but also for the lungs. Festivals are celebrated there, marriages are held, babies are born, and the infirm and the old die. There is no privacy, no separate toilet, no separate bath. Many slums have neither a water tap nor electricity. Where there are no drains, water stagnates in the nearest depressions, resulting in filth and strench, which serves as a breeding place for flies and mosquitoes. Some slum-dwellers augment their income by keeping some poultry, or a goat or two, a cow or a buffalo, or a few pigs and donkeys. These birds and animals are all integrals of the slum population, and when their waste is dumped near the slum itself, it adds to dirt and stink, making the slum area prone to physical disorders and diseases among its inhabitants.

Through the vote-catching strategy of the former Government of Madhya Pradesh, some slums have shown signs of minor improvements. Instead of shifting the slum-dwellers to other localities and housing them by constructing tenements planned for the economically weaker sections of the society, which could cost the Government both money and unpopularity, the Government considered it expedient to confer upon each jhuggi owner *pattas* of legal ownership, one single-point connection of free electricity, and a single community municipal water tap or a hand-pump, but did not provide proper drains and community toilets. Ownership rights obliterated the apprehension of being shifted elsewhere and gave legality to these unauthorised structures on encroached land, and several jhuggi-dwellers started improving both the exterior and the interior of their abodes. With rising incomes, some of them brought into their jhuggis a black and white TV set or transistor, a steel bed with mosquito nets, stainless steel utensils, and even a pressure cooker.

In spite of material possessions—to which may be added a watch, a bicycle, readymade garments for men and children, and a couple of silver ornaments for women—the slum-dwellers are largely illiterate, superstitious, quarrelsome, and an easy prey to the temptations of drinking, drug addiction, gambling, petty crime, and vice. The Malthusian theory of population was largely applicable to the slum-dwellers a few decades before. With publicity and persuasion by family planning workers, many of the slum-dwellers have gradually come round to the idea of planning a family. Whether this change is due to the emergence of a rational outlook among them, or whether there is the allure of cash and other incentives, is open to question.

During her survey of Hoshangabad city, the writer has identified 9 slum areas for the purpose of the present study. Table 14 indicates their location and their approximate population.

Table 14

The Slums of Hoshangabad Location and Population

1990

Location	*Approximate population*
Malakheri	1,010
New Tube Well, Govindpura	220
Narainganj	120
Bhilpura	75
Jumerati, Ward 5	60
Between Jumerati and Kori Mohalla	55
Ramganj	45
Rajghat Road	40
Karbala Road	25
Total	1,650

Source : Personal Investigation.

The largest slum, Malakheri (population around 1,010), is about 5 kilometres way from the city on Piparia Road, with a mixed population of Hindus and Muslims, the former being in a majority. The Hindus include the higher and the lower castes—Brahmins, Yadavs (originally cowherds), Dhobis (originally washermen), and Gonds (primitive tribals). The second largest slums (population about 220), located near the new tube well and also near Government Home Science College, comes under Municipal Ward, 17, and is mostly populated by Chamars (originally skin and hide workers) who call themselves Jatavs. The third in rank according to population (nearly 120) it Naraingani in Municipal Ward 6. It has also a mixed population of Hindus and Muslims, with Nais (Barbers) in a majority, the others being Thakurs and Dhimars. The slum, ranking fourth in terms of population (almost 75), is officially named in municipal records as Bhilpura Ward. It is also a mixed slum of Hindus and Muslims, populated largely by Dhimars (originally fishermen), Kumhars (Potters), and Manjhis (boatmen).

The fifth slum (population approximately 60) lies in Jumerati Mohalla under Municipal Ward 5, and is populated by tribals and Harijans. The sixth slum (population nearly 55) is situated between Jumerati Mohalla and Kori Mohalla. Its population comprises of Dhimars, Basors, and Nais. The seventh slum (population around 45) comes under Ramganj municipal Ward 7 and consists exclusively of Harijans. The eighth slum (population about 40) is situated at Ramghat Road and is inhabited by Harijans and Dhimars. The last and the smallest slum (population about 25) is situated on Government grasslands, near Normal School, Karbala Road, and houses Dhimars and Rekwars.

Existing literature

There is no dearth of literature on population as well as family planning. Most of it is on micro level and deals with the global population situation in general terms. Some studies discuss and evaluate family planning and programmes on an all-India basis. Only a few are micro studies related either to urban or rural areas. Among population studies on the global level, mention may be made of a few useful ones. The Report of the commission on Population Growth and the American Future deals with the causes and possible future consequences of unrestricted population growth in American society.[1] Much of what has been written is also applicable to India.

P.R. Ehrlich and A.H. Ehrlich jointly study in detail the relationship between population and the environment, and advocate immediate action to avert an ecological crisis caused by overpopulation.[2] The study of the correlation between overpopulation and ecological imbalance is also relevant in the context of the prevailing Indian scene.

David M. Heer has written a short, well-organised and coherent analysis of the factors leadingtopopulation explosion.[3] Although Heer does not discuss India in detail, the reader can easily recognise that the major factors contributing to the population boom are similar to those in India. Donella Meadows and her co-authors predict catastrophic consequences for the world's population if demands for resources continue to expand.[4] This is partially true for a developing country like India, because much of her resources are yet to be fully exploited and developed. However, caution is necessary so that future generations are not put to trouble.

As regards planned parenthood, L.A. Westoff and C.F. Westoff offer a complete discussion of contraceptive methods and examine the current trends in fertility and family planning. They also make a balanced projection in the future of population growth

---

1. "Population Growth and America's Future", *Family Planning Perspective,* No. 3, 1971.
2. Paul R. Ehrlich and Anne H. Ehrlich, *Population, Resources, Environment, Issues on Human Ecology,* W.H. Freeman, San Francisco, 1987.
3. David M. Heer, *Society and Population,* Prentice-Hall, Englewood Cliffs, New Jersey, 1978.
4. Donella Meadows and Others, *The Limits to Growth,* Universe, New York, 1980.

and the possible social consequences.[5] Similarly, the United Nations conducted a study in fertility and family planning, but it is related to Europe around 1970 and is not very useful in the Indian socio-economic scenario of today.[6] R.H. Boyd's book is still older (1947) and bears little relevance to conditions prevailing today.[7]

R.G. Patter's research paper on birth interval dynamics deals with the spacing of children, which is a vital component of planned parenthood and the health of both the mother and the baby.[8] R.G. Ridker has contributed a valuable essay on the optimum size of the family and has also examined the efficacy of current family planning programmes.[9] The Report of the Third International Conference in planned Parenthood held in 1952 is a pioneer study and deals with the global situation, with only a perfunctory reference to India. Kumudni Dandekar has written exhaustively on the little known aspect of family planning, namely, communication.[10]

The Indian Year book provides valuable information on family welfare programmes in India, but it lacks insight and perception with reference to the individual States comprising the Indian Union. Similarly, the Department of Family Planning in New Delhi used to disseminate statistical information on family planning in India, but the periodicity of its publications was erratic, and not regular. A. Sengupta's article on the rhythm method in exploring the libido pattern in women is quite an interesting reading material.[11] C.B. Mamoria's book seeks to

5. L.A. Westoff and C.F. Westoff, *From Now to Zero*, Little, Brown, Boston, 1981.
6. United Nations, *Population Studies,* No. 58, New York, 1976.
7. R.H. Boyd, *Controlled Parenthood,* Universe, New York, 1976.
8. R.G. Patter, "A Case Study of Birth Interval Dynamics, *Population Studies,* vol. 19, July 1965.
9. R.G. Ridker, "Desired Family Size and the Efficacy of Current Planning Programmes," *Population Studies,* vol. 23, 1963.
10. Kumudni Dandekar, *Communication in Family Planning,* Asia Publishing House, New York, 1977.
11. A Sengupta, "A Study of the Rhythm Method in Exploring the Pattern of libido in human Female", *Journal of Family Welfare,* vol. 4, No. 3, 1979.

correlate population and family planning. It is a fairly helpful study, though somewhat antiquated.[12] C. Chandrasekharan studies only a single aspect in family planning, namely, the physiological factors affecting fertility in India, but his research reveals many corners which were hitherto rather obscure, and reiterates the fundamental necessity of health of husband, wife, and children.[13] K.G. Krishnamurthy's work on research and research problems in India is useful of students researching in India.[14]

Coming to regional studies, one of the early works is that of S.N. Agarwal who conducted a study on fertility control through contraceptives with Delhi as his universe of study. The work has now become out of date, as more than two decades have elapsed since its publication, and fertility control methods have become much more advanced than they were in 1958.[15] J.R. Lele and Tara Kanitkar investigated fertility and family planning in Greater Bombay against the residential backdrop.[16] What is remarkable about the paper is that it highlights the influence of localities—the socio-economic environment—on the total or partial acceptance or rejection of controlled parenthood by a group of people.

M.E. Opler's essay, contributed to *Fact and Theory in Social Science* analysis population control programmes in rural India in the context of culture. The culture context is significant, since most rural-based cultures still encourage the birth of babies,

---

12. C.B. Mamoria, *Population and Family Planning in India,* Kitab Mahal, Allahabad, 1963.
13. C. Chandrasekharan, *Physiological Factors Affecting Fertility in India,* Demographic Training and Research Centre, Bombay, 1979.
14. K.G. Krishnamurthy, *Research in Family Planning in India,* Sterling Publishers, New Delhi, 1978.
15. S.N. Agarwal, "Fertility Control Through Contraceptives : Results of Delhi Study", *Family Planning News,* vol. I, No. 2, July 1958.
16. J.R. Lele and Tara Kanitkar, "Residence Background and Fertility to greater Bombay", *Population Studies,* vol. 28, No. 2, July 1974.

while others do not frown upon restricted births.[17] The Delhi-based Programme Evaluation Organisation's publication is a factual evaluation of the family planning programme in 1970.[18] If any organisation undertakes and publishes an evaluation of family planning and family welfare programmes, initiated and implemented in the various States of India on a year to year basis, the burden on the research student will be considerably lightened.

S. Krishnakumar focuses his attention on family planning at Ernakulam in Kerala in a readable manner and brings out the initial difficulties encountered by motivators and family planning acceptors.[19] The only study relating to Bhopal is Dr. Firoza Ansari's unpublished Ph.D. thesis, which is an in-depth study of family planning, as accepted and practised by the Muslim community in urban Bhopal, based on extensive field work.[20]

Objectives of the study

The main objectives of the study are enumerated as under :

(i) To study the marital status, level of education, and occupation of the slum-dwellers, so as to establish a proper perspective;

(ii) To ascertain the economic status of slum-families with a view to discover any correlation between income and family planning;

(iii) To investigate their responses to planned parenthood which include the age of marriage, the age-difference

---

17. E.W. Count and G. Baules, Eds., *Fact and Theory in Social Science*, Syracuse University Press, Syracuse, 1974.
18. *Family Planning Programme : An Evaluation,* Programme Evaluation Organisation, New Delhi, 1970.
19. S. Krishnakumar, *The Story of the Ernakulam Experiment in Family Planning,* Government of Kerala Cochin, 1971.
20. Firoza Ansari, *Family Planning Among Muslims in Bhopal : A Study in Social Change,* Unpublished Ph. D. Thesis, Bhopal University, Bhopal, 1983.

between husband and wife, the number of children per slum family, and allied factors;

(iv) To inquire into the methods of family planning preferred by slum families—natural methods, biological methods, chemical methods, mechanical methods, or surgical methods;

(v) To ascertain the impact of family planning on the individual behaviour and health of adopters of planned parenthood;

(vi) To examine the attitude of slum elders towards family planning and to identify the decision-makers in family welfare;

(vii) To assess the motivating factors leading to the acceptance of family planning—incentives or free will; and finally;

(viii) To consider what social change family planning has effected among its adopters in the slums.

The universe

The nine slum areas identified by the writer, with varying population in terms of numbers, castes and communities, scattered in different parts of Hoshangabad, a historical town on the banks of the holy Narmada, near Bhopal, constitute the universe of study.

Study design

Procedural specificity and thorough observation of the study design are indispensable for any investigation. A study design refers to the logical manner in which the units of the study are compared and analysed for the purpose of making generalisations. In this investigation, a description of the study design is enumerated as under :

The hypothesis is a primary and integral part of any social investigation, as it focuses the process of data collection and other related activities of social research. The main hypothesis of the present study is that the common belief about the slum-dwellers breeding fast and resisting social change is no longer tenable in the context of family planning programmes as operating at present.

To determine whether the hypothesis is probably true or not, some related verifiable hypothetical propositions have been formulated and presented as under :

(i) The level of education and family planning are interlinked.

(ii) Family income is a contributory factor in family welfare.

(iii) Adults, whether externally motivated or self-motivated, adopt family planning, the age at which they married and the age-difference between the spouses being immaterial.

(iv) Partners in marriage, adopting planned parenthood, who have more children than they desire tend to prefer surgical methods, while others go in for mechanical ones.

(v) The adoption of family planning neither affects the sex life of the couple not causes permanent discomfort.

(vi) The initial reaction to family planning is one of apprehension and embarrassment.

(vii) The elders in the slums have begun to realise the benefits of limiting a family.

(viii) The final decision to adopt family planning is that of the couples themselves.

(ix) The advantages resulting from family planning are the chief motivating factors, while incentives serve as compensation for working time or days lost by the couple.

Research methodology

The present study is based largely on primary data, and partly on secondary data. The source of primary data is field work consisting of visits to slum areas for on-the-spot study of the condition of families living there and include responses of family planning acceptors to a carefully prepared interview schedule, as well as visits to family planning and health centres in Hoshangabad city to study their clientele, performance, achievements, and shortfalls. The statistics so collected have been carefully sorted out and presented in a tabular form. The data in each table are then analysed and interpreted within their relevant framework so as to deduce factual conclusions.

Secondary data covers a careful study of existing literature on family planning in India and abroad, including official documents released by organisations actively involved in family welfare programmes as well as specialised writing—in the form of books, studies, reports, and articles appearing in periodicals—of scholars knowledgeable in the contribution of family welfare to the developmental policies and programmes of India.

Where necessary, events and their historical relevance to the family welfare movement have been briefly described. In this way, the study is both descriptive and diagnostic. Where comments have been made on the achievements and pitfalls of the movement and suggestions offered to minimise or eliminate the discrepancies and defects in the implementation of family welfare programmes, the study is also critical and creative.

Limitations

Though there has been a conscious effort to maintain scientific orientation and reliability of the data at every step of the investigation, the validity of the present findings may not be fully applicable to the slum areas of the other districts of Madhya Pradesh and other States. In spite of no effort being spared to make the study quite comprehensive, the paucity of time and lack of resources have rendered the incorporation of all aspects impracticable. Yet the findings of this investigation may be combined with similar studies which may contribute, in some measure, to the emergence of a general theory.

Chapter II

FAMILY PLANNING IN PERSPECTIVE

India may have something to learn from China which seems determined to bring down its birth rate, using fairly stringent disincentives (if necessary) along with incentives. The latest step in this direction is the decision to impose a stiff fine—no less than three times the average local income—on couples who have more than one child. In the case of those who have a third child, the fine will be awhopping six times the average annual income. The decision, which was announced in Shanghai and will doubtless be enforced in every city and town, is evidently the Government's reaction to the recently reported action of a woman party cadre in opting for a second child in defiance of the one-child norm which has been in force for quite some years, exemptions from it being allowed only to couples in rural areas whose first child happens to be a girl. There is no such exemption in urban areas, irrespective of the firstborn's sex, and the party cadre who craved for a son decided to have for a second child in the face of stern party suggestions to terminate her pregnancy.

Such rigorousness will, of course, be anathema to those who support the concept of free choice in such personal matters, and, particularly, to those who are opposed to abortion, but it certainly makes sense from the perspective of the need to arrest wild population growth. However harsh, the proposed fine should effectively deter couples from violating the one-child norm and will, in the long run, prove beneficial to them as, indeed, to China's entire population. The willingness of the Chinese authorities to employ such disincentives, risking short-term unpopularity for the sake of the ultimate good of all, is worth serious consideration in this country, especially since reliable projections indicate that the population will double to 1,770 million by the year 2025, and will exceed that of China only a very few years later. But for some reason, those in charge of India's family planning programmes seem still reluctant to go in for even the slightest disincentive, choosing instead to place their entire trust in gentle persuasion which smacks of criminal naivete. With an annual population growth rate of 2.08 per cent, against China's 1.38 per cent, and the family planning programme admitted by all to be in a state of somnolence, it is high time the Government get off the fence and bestirred itself to consider active disincentives, also in order to arrest India's galloping birth rate.[1]

India, however, has the distinction of being the first country in the world to launch a nation-wide family planning programme with full Government support. It is of interest to study the historical evolution of her ante-natalist policy and to critically assess the programmes undertaken in pursuance of this policy in the light of achievements over the years.

The pre-independence period

The British rulers of the country were not interested in formulating any population policy for India, nor were they in favour of the birth control movement which had started making its presence felt. As pointed out by Chandrasekhar, till the early

1. "Example from China", Third editorial, *The Statesman*, New Delhi, 22 August 1990, p. 6.

twenties the British measured the prosperity of their rule, to some extent, by the magnitude of the net addition to India's population.[2] The degree of satisfaction over and the justification of the British rule in India was directly in proportion to the substantial increase in the population that the Census revealed every decade. The absence of support from the British rulers to the birth control movement was, firstly, because in their own homeland the birth control issue was itself controversial, and secondly, because the general policy of the British was to keep away from any measures which would be considered by the Indians as an intrusion on their own traditions, customs, values, and beliefs.

A section of the intellectual elite among the Indians showed some concern about the population issue during the period between the two World Wars. The 1931 Census indicated that the intercesal increase was much higher than during the earlier decade, and there was much difference of opinion regarding whether India was over-populated or not. The neo-Malthusians were of the opinion that a smaller population would mean better living conditions for the masses. In 1935, the Indian National Congress set up a National Planning Committee under the chairmanship of Jawaharlal Nehru.

The National Planning Committee agreed with the view that the size of the Indian population is a basic issue in national economic planning in so far as its unrestricted increase in proportion to means of subsistence affects adversely the standard of living, and tends to defeat many social and ameliorative measures. The problem has been fundamentally caused by the lack of all-round coordinated economic development. While measures for the improvement of the quality of the population and limiting excessive population pressure are necessary, the basic solution of the present disparity between population and standard of living lies in the economic progress of the country on a comprehensive and planned basis.

---

2. Chandrasekhar, S., *India's Population,* 1950, p. 12.

In the interest of social economy, family happiness and national planning, family planning and limitations of children are essential and the State should adopt a policy to encourage these. It is desirable to lay stress on self-control and also to spread knowledge of cheap and safe methods of birth control. Birth control clinics should be established and other necessary measures taken in this behalf to prevent the use of harmful methods.

The National Planning Committee recommended that a gradual rising of the marriage age and discouragement of polygamy are desirable in the interest of the limitations of the size of the family. The Committee was also of the view that a eugenic programme should include the sterilisation of persons suffering from transmissible disease of a serious nature such as insanity or epilepsy. The Committee also emphasised that the maintenance of vital statistics and the carrying out of periodic demographic surveys on comprehensive lines are necessary, and an appropriate machinery should be devised for the purpose.

Mahatma Gandhi's views on planned parenthood

The impact of Gandhiji's views on birth control also need to be taken into account because he exercised a strong influence over the Indian masses, not only in the political field but also in the other areas of human life. Though Gandhiji accepted the need for birth control, it was advocated on ethical and moral grounds, for he maintained that planned parenthood would improve the moral fibre and the physical health of the individual. On the same ethical and moral grounds, he was against any artificial means of contraception, but he lent his full support to brahmacharya or abstinence. He declared that there could be no two opinions about the necessity for birth control. But the only method handed down from ages past is self-control or brahmacharya. It is an infallible sovereign remedy, doing good to those who practise it. The union is meant not for pleasure but for bringing forth progeny. He, however, conceded that another method, which had an appeal for him, was the rhythm method based on avoidance of sexual union during unsafe period, that is, when conception was likely to occur. Gandhiji's views on whether or not India was over-populated are also noteworthy. He believed that, if all laboured for their bread, there would be enough food and leisure for all, and there would be no cry of over-population, no disease, and no misery. His strong views on the enslavement of Indians by the British also made him advise his people that it was their duty to suspend bringing forth heirs to our slavery.

The post-independence period

Family planning has to be pursued vigorously as a wholly voluntary programme and as an integral part of a comprehensive policy concerning education, health, maternity and child-care, family welfare, women's rights, and nutrition. The vital importance of family planning lies in the fact that it is a means of individual and national development and well-being. The Government is totally committed to the family welfare programme and will spare no efforts to motivate the people to accept it voluntarily in their own interest and in the interest of the society.

Family planning has, however, to be lifted from its old and narrow concept and given its proper place in the overall programmes of welfare, particularly those which are designed to protect and promote the health of mothers and children. It must become a part of the total concept of positive health. At the same time, it must find meaningful integration with other welfare programmes, viz., nutrition, education, employment, and women's welfare. It would be our endeavour to bring about this integration to a greater degree.

The change in the name of the programme from family planning to family welfare is a reflection of the Government's anxiety to promote the total welfare of the family and the society. The intention is to take the programme forward in the real sense as an investment in man. In this task, there is no room for compulsion. Coercion in the area of family welfare must be ruled out for all times to come. The approach is educational and wholly voluntary. There should, however, be no slackening of efforts in this direction.

The Government attaches the highest importance to the dignity of the citizen and to his right to determine the size of his family. By the large, the people of India are conscious of the importance of responsible parenthood. Given the necessary information and adequate services, they will accept the small family norm. Promotion must be given to all methods with equal emphasis, and it should be left to every family to decide what method of contraception it would like to adopt. Employees of the Union Government, State Governments, autonomous bodies, local bodies, and others, are expected to set an example and to adopt the small-family norm.

In a federal system, the sharing of Central resources with the States is a matter of considerable importance. Family planning and population is a subject in the concurrent list, yet the implementation of the family welfare programme is very much the responsibility of the Government of India.

Health education

There is no doubt that population control is necessary, but merely controlling the population is not going to make the people healthy. Health also is a means to an end, the end being the happiness of the people of this country as a whole. No person can hope to enjoy happiness if he is not healthy. Therefore it is really very necessary that conditions should be created to enable him to keep healthy. Again, it is not possible for a person to keep healthy at the cost of somebody else, unless one cooperates in this task. Therefore, it is imperative that people are educated how to maintain their health.

Population explosion

Population explosion has become a serious problem in India because of poverty and scarce means of production which are not available to every person. If adequate means of production had been available for every person, population would have not been a problem. As matter of fact, every person produces more than he needs if given the proper opportunity of work. Moreover, when everybody has work and is happy, population control comes in automatically on account of several factors including psychological and physiological processes. If population goes on increasing at the rate it has been growing, all our programmes for giving work and providing means of production would be rendered futile. It is, therefore, most vital that we should control the population and look upon population control as a major programme.

The emergency period of 1975-77

During the past few years, family planning became rather a menace to the people, because it was being forced on them, especially the programme of tubectomy and vasectomy. It was being done indiscriminately. That is what happens if it is done only in order to count the heads. If it is decided that so many men have to be vasectomised so that the growth rate of the population goes down, then those who have to carry it out would only think about the number of people, and not about the kind of people concerned. That is what actually happened. It meant a lot of oppression on the poor, mainly because nobody was going to force the rich people to offer themselves for this. It is only the poor people who could be forced to do it. It is obvious that we cannot have a programme for the welfare of the people by means of coercion because coercion has its own limits.

But in any programme of health coercion will not help. If we make a person do exercises compulsorily for his bodily health, he will somehow do it, because he has got to do it, otherwise he will have to pay a price for it. People have, therefore, to be educated about the advantages of the exercises and have to be shown how those exercise can be taken without any discomfort and how they can be of great advantage. That is why the policy of the Government is to have family planning and population control as vigorously as possible on a voluntary basis. If the task is attended to by all concerned in the right spirit, there will be proper response from people. When people take to it willingly, the programme will give much better results, and it will be done in a more effective manner. It will then also result in the welfare of the people.

Family welfare

Family welfare denotes a wider field of activity. Whatever development we want in the society depends upon the capacity of the people to do their work efficiently, so that they increase their productive capacity in the field of work that they take up. If that is to be done, health becomes the preliminary condition. Unless a person enjoys fairly good health, it will not be possible for him to do his work efficiently. It is, therefore, necessary for us to see that the people of India are enabled to maintain their health in a fairly good manner so that they are able to pursue their work and professions efficiently and to lead healthy lives.

Family planning perspective

The family planning programme, since its very inception in 1952, has been the responsibility of the Ministry of Health. It began very modestly, indeed, with the creation of a Family Planning Cell in the Planning and Development Section of the Directorate—General of Health Services in April 1952. The first Officer on Special Duty to be in charge of the programme was appointed in March 1956 : his designation was later changed to Director of Family Planning. At the State level, family planning officers were appointed, and they were responsible for the actual implementation of the programme.

In 1966, several important developments concerning the family planning programme took place. A full-fledged Department of Family Planning was established within the Ministry which was re-designated as the Ministry of Health and Family Planning and a Minister of Cabinet rank was placed in its charge. The Central Family Planning Council, with the Minister of Health and Family Planning as its Chairman, was set up in 1966.

Till 1973-74, the Department of Family Planning was headed by the Secretary of Health and Family Planning. The Additional Secretary, Family Planning, looked after the administrative wing, while the Commissioner, Family Planning and Maternal and Child Health, was in charge of the technical wing. The marketing executive held independent charge for the implementation of the scheme for the commercial distribution of Nirodh. In 1974-75, the post of the Commissioner of Family Planning was elevated to the level of the Joint Secretary.

Since its inception in 1952, the family planning programme has undergone several revisions which, despite severe criticism, show that those who administer the programme are willing to learn from experience. It is obvious that rigidity in the implementation of the programme would not have been the correct stance to adopt.

The family planning programme in India started with a very cautious approach. The natural method of family planning (the rhythm method) was also considered to be the most appropriate for the Indian masses, and this method was widely propagated. Since India was the first country in the world to adopt family planning as a nation-wide programme, there was no model that she could follow. The only model available for this purpose was the one used by the Planned Parenthood Organisations in the West, which set up family planning clinics, and those who needed family planning were expected to take advantage of these facilities. The limitations of such an approach may well be imagined. The approach is based on the assumption that those who need family planning would visit such clinics without any hesitation. Such an assumption, however, ruled out the need to educate the people. Moreover, the planned parenthood model leans heavily in favour of services for women rather than for the couple. It also leans heavily on medical personnel, which was, and is, rather scarce in India. This "clinic approach", as it was called, could reach only a relatively small fraction of the people, and could not make much impact on birth rates. The approach was, therefore, not considered suitable for a developing country like India. Hence, the need for the adoption of "the extension approach" to family planning was soon realised.

The emphasis on the need for group acceptance of family planning recognised the fact that individuals do not live in a vacuum but are greatly influenced by the group in which they live. It is difficult for individuals to accept new forms of behaviour unless they are acceptable to their group as a whole. If family planning is to be adopted by individual couples, they would do so more easily if the idea of family planning is acceptable to their group. It is, therefore, necessary to build up group and community support for the programme rather than work with individuals and expect them to adopt family planning by becoming "rebels" or "deviants".

Family planning services and supplies

It is obvious that if a couple has to practise family planning, knowledge about family planning is essential—knowledge that it is possible to prevent conception, knowledge about the various methods of contraception so that the most suitable method be chosen, and knowledge about where such methods are available.

Easy availability of supplies and services is also essential if couples are to practise family planning successfully. It is true that if motivation for family planning is strong enough, a couple would seek out the sources of supplies an services even if they are not easily available. But such strong motivation is not always forthcoming. It is better, therefore, to facilitate the practice of family planning by removing both physical and psychological barriers associated with the usual sources of supplies and services for that purpose. If a family planning centre is at a considerable distance and the clinical atmosphere is quite imposing, both these factors may act as barriers to the acceptance of the family planning programme.

Family planning service is likely to succeed if the clinics are associated with maternity and child health work, or with centres which provide medical aid and welfare services. The principle of integration of family planning services with maternal and child health services has thus been accepted almost since the beginning of the family planning programme. Confidence can be created only by providing both preventive and curative medical services for children. It is also obvious that, while providing such services, health workers may approach mothers for family planning with greater credibility.

It is generally claimed that India has always adopted the "cafeteria approach" and continues to do so. Though this implies that all available methods of contraception are offered to the people with the choice left to them, in actual practice it is found that each method of contraception has received varying emphasis at different times. These methods have included the rhythm method, the diaphragm and jelly method, foam tablets, the condom, the intra-uterine device (IUD), male and female sterilisation.

Population education for the younger generation is also accepted as a supportive measure, so that the young might grow up with a greater awareness of the population problem and realisation of their national responsibility. Education and motivation of men and women involve all departments in the family planning programme, including the responsibility of bringing cases for sterilisation. The medical services concentrated on providing services. Targets were given to school teachers, Patwaris, Gramsevaks, Gram Panchayats. Directives were given to all "eligible" employees of the State Governments to undergo sterilisation by a certain date. Special prizes are awarded to districts for good performance in family planning and integration of health and family planning services.

Any legislation which compels people to get sterilised goes against the voluntary principle in family planning affirmed in the World Population Conference at Bucharest. Consistent with the Proclamation of the International Conference on Human Rights, the Declaration of Progress and Development, the relevant targets of the Second United Nations Development Decade, and other international instruments on the subject, the Conference recommended that all countries must respect and ensure, regardless of their overall demographic goals, the right of persons to determine in a free, informed and responsible manner the number and spacing of their children.

The new nomenclature

The family planning programme was renamed as the family welfare programme to make it more acceptable and to denote that it had a wider base, so that it could include various measures of family welfare for the improvement of the quality of human life. The wider policy of family welfare covered education, health, maternity and child care, family planning, and nutrition.

India adopted the family planning programme on a national scale with the expectation that a lower rate of population increase would aid economic and social advancement. Therefore, the Government sponsored various birth control measures. The programme changed over time from a pure and simple clinical approach to extension education, and from that to mass sterilization camps, and from such camps to small camps which Would be managed with less difficulty. This new basis of the programme was reflected in its epidemiological base as well as its technological component. These two, combined together, determined its organisational structure and the strategies which were adopted to reduce population growth.

The Government's approach to population control was heavily dependent upon the type of technology used. It first put its hopes on IUCD (Intra Ulterine Contraceptive Device); and, when that did not bear fruit, it shifted emphasis on to sterilisations. This required a massive structure, which was built up with heavy investment. By 1968, apart from the non-technical staff, an organisation employing 1,25,000 technical personnel was ready for India's Family Planning Programme.[3] Despite this, the result was much below expectations. To catch up with the targets, one of the strategies adopted within the programme was the use of communication technology for propagating the message of family planning and for motivating people to accept the small family as a norm. The importance of education and motivation through

---

3. Government of India, Department of Family Planning, "Indian Family Planning Programme Since 1965", New Delhi, 1968, p. 43.

communication was brought into the light only when the traditional clinical approach was found to be inadequate. From the Third Plan onwards, communication had become a part and parcel of the family planning programme

There has been a massive financial allotment for communication in various Five-Year Plans. There has been extensive use of various media of mass communication from mass media to integrated media. Almost all methods of communication have been used. The Government has constituted communication activities. Along with the decision to establish mass media and extension services for person-to-person communication, special units of mass communication were created at the Central and State levels within the Department of Health and Family Planning. These were provided with staff, equipment and vehicles. Inputs were also provided to the Central Ministry of Information and Broadcasting for the purpose of promoting family planning among the people Last but not the least, the Government also took the help of foreign communications experts. Family planning communication policy and programme cannot be independent of the overall policies of the family planning programme which places family planning at the centre of its planning process and attempts at carrying it forward with the rest of the developmental programmes, and not in isolation.

To implement such a policy, the entire structure of the family planning programme will have to be dismantled and reorganised so that the family planning programme comes down from its domineering heights and becomes a part of the Government health services. Within the new structure, a new set of norms have to be evolved to give priority to areas which hitherto have been neglected, like maternal and child health, water supply and sanitation, immunisation and other nutrition programmes, along with family planning services. It is only within this new policy framework and structure of the family planning programme that the implementation of a rational family planning communication policy is feasible.

Changes in family size arise from within the situation which includes the objective socio-economic environment and value system which confront the masses. The idea of a child as a consumption unit rather than an investment may be relevant for the upper strata of our society. But for the people family size is very much determined by old age security and land-holding. Education, especially the education of women, is of paramount importance. If the women get educated and economically independent, they can decide the family size themselves without depending on the dominating members of the family like the husband, father-in-law, or mother-in-law.[4]

Family welfare

Family welfare programme, which is an essential part of the strategy of enlarging welfare is being implemented as a wholly voluntary programme and as an integral part of the overall strategy of growth covering health, maternity and child care, family welfare, women's rights and nutrition. The salient features of the strategy are : (i) intensified efforts to spread awareness and information through imaginative use of multi-media and interpersonal communication; (ii) provision of services and supplies as close to the doorsteps of the acceptors as possible; (iii) development of facilities for rapid increase in female literacy; (iv) population education to the young in schools and colleges as well as those out of schools; (v) assistance and support of the elected representatives of the people, (vi) proper linkages with other Ministries and Departments concerned (vii) incentives to individual acceptors and State Governments, and (viii) close monitoring and follow-up of the programme at all levels.

Though officially the family planning programme in India was launched in 1952, the birth control movement in the country is older than that. The first two birth control clinics anywhere in the world were established in Karnataka as far back as in 1930. In those days, birth control was not talked about freely. In the West as well as in India, some people did practise it, but they

---

4. Pati, R.N., *Population, Family, and Culture,* 1987, pp. 161.

belonged to the elite. Some traditional methods of contraception were used in India, but there was no such thing as a Government-sponsored organised family planning programme. There was, however, a good deal of consciousness among the enlightened people in the country that, in the interest of happily family life and the well-being of the community, contraception facilities should be provided to those who wanted them. The establishment of the two clinics in Karnataka in 1930 is indicative of this.

Family welfare under Five-Year Plans

With the launching of the First Plan, India entered the era of planning. In recognition of the fact that a rapidly growing population would be a hindrance in raising the standards of living of the people, family planning was adopted as an official programme in 1952. During the First and Second Plans, the programme was taken up in a modest way with clinical approach and the stress was mainly on research in the Field of demography, communication, physiology of reproduction, and motivation. Centres were also established in certain areas for providing clinical services and advice on family planning to those who came to seek it.

The programme was reorganised in the Third Plan and the "clinical approach" adopted so far was supplemented by the "extension approach" under which the message, services and supplies of contraceptives were sought to be made available to the people on a cafeteria basis in regard to adoption of the methods. A full-fledged Department of Family Planning was created at the Centre in 1966, and the programme was reorganised and made target-oriented on the basis of a report of a sub-committee. In the Fourth and Fifth Plans, the programme was accorded a very high priority. During these years, the programme underwent great expansion, consolidation and integration of family planning with maternal and child health care. As a result of independent evaluation of the programme, important changes were introduced in it to make it more responsive to the larger needs of the people. These changes embraced almost all areas relevant to family planning, mass education and motivation, services and supplies, training of workers, research and evaluation, association of voluntary organisations with the programme, and systematic involvement in it of the organised sector of industry and their employers.

For disseminating information and educating people about family welfare, press, films, radio and television, oral and visual communication media like song and drama troupes and interpersonal communication through a network of media and extension workers are being used extensively. Besides the eligible couples, an effort is also being made to reach potentially important sections of population to motivate them to accept small-family norm when they reach the reproductive stage. Population education has been introduced in the formal school and university system in the country. With the cooperation and assistance of official and non-official agencies working in the country for development programmes, like trade unions, cooperatives and panchayats, their training programmes are being used for introducing population education through non-formal channels.

Implementation machinery

The programmes are implemented through the State Governments for which cent per cent Central assistance is provided. In rural areas, the programme is being further extended through a network of primary health centres and sub-centres. The Sixth Plan envisaged the establishment of 37,940 additional sub-centres during 1980-85, of which about 35,774 sub-centres have been established and it was proposed to establish another 54,883 sub-centres during the Seventh Plan. Maternal and child health care and expanded programme of immunisation are also a part of the family welfare programme.

Performance

Since the inception of programme, 5.38 lakh sterilisations and 186 lakh IUD insertions have been done, giving a rate of 71.2 per thousand population for sterilisation and 24.6 for IUD insertions upto 31 March 1986.

Nirodh is sold under the commercial scheme operated through a network of over 3 lakh retail shops by 12 leading consumer goods marketing companies in India. Under the free distribution scheme, Nirodh, diaphragms, jelly cream tubes, and foam tablets are also distributed.

The oral pill programme was extended to all the urban centres, including those run by local bodies and voluntary organisations and those primary health centres where the programme could be monitored and patients followed up. The pills are now being distributed through 22,015 centres functioning in the rural and urban areas of the country.

Impact of the programme

It is estimated that 35 per cent of 12.94 crore eligible couples whose wives are in the reproductive age-group 15-44 were protected by one or the other of the approved methods of family welfare as on 31 March, 1986. As a result of the work done up to 31 March, 1986, estimated 746 lakh births have been averted. These figures are provisional.

Medical termination of pregnancy

The programme of medical termination of pregnancy through well trained doctors in well-equipped approved hospitals is essentially a health care measure. But in a way it supplements the family welfare programme as it provides for legalised abortion in caes of contraceptive failures also. A good proportion of the acceptors of abortion go in for some form of contraception like sterilisation or IUD. The Medical Termination of Pregnancy Act 1971 is in operation since April, 1972.

Maternal and child health programme

Care of mothers and children, the vulnerable groups of the society, plays a pivotal role in family welfare programme. The maternity and child health programmes (MCH) are directed towards effective ante-natal care, ensuring safe and aseptic delivery and apporpriate post-natal care, initiation and maintenance of breast feeding, timely immunisation against common infectious diseases, control of diarrhoea, attention to growth, and provision of basic medical care.

Infrastructure of health is being extended and manpower is being trained to achieve these objectives of MCH care. To provide specialised paediatric care, paediatric units in districts, sub-divisional hospitals and newly set-up units of district hospitals have been and are being equipped. A sum of Rs. 15.30 crore was provided during 1986-87 for procurement of vaccines and MCH drugs for immunising children and mothers against diseases and preventing nutritional anaemia. An amount of Rs. 400 crore was provided for the programme of control of diarrhoeal diseases among children through rehydration therapy during 1986-87, and there was a provision of Rs. 25 crore for this new programme during the Seventh Plan.

Training of multipurpose workers

To ensure package of health and family welfare services at the peripheral level, multipurpose workers are being trained. The training was expected to be completed in all the districts during the Sixth Plan period. Re-training of district level medical officers and the key trainees is organised at seven central training institutions, and that of medical officers of primary health centres and block extension educators at 47 health and family planning training centres. The para medical staff of the block is trained at these primary health centres.

Special schemes

Four schemes, namely, (i) all India hospitals post-partum programme at district and sub-district level hospitals and PAP smear test facilities in medical colleges selected for the purpose; (ii) revamping of organisational set-up in urban slums of the country; (iii) sterilisation beds scheme; and (iv) renovation of IUD room at rural family welfare centres attached to primary health centres, are being implemented as special schemes.

The post-partum programme is a maternity-centred and

hospital-based approach to family welfare programme, and now covers 554 medical institutions at national, State, and district levels. These include 104 medical colleges, and two postgraduate institutions. Besides, 25 medical colleges are also implementing PAP smear test facilities programme for early detection of cervical cancer among acceptors of family welfare methods.

The purpose of extension of the post-partum programme to sub-district hospitals is to provide the maternal and child health care services in rural and semi-urban areas so as to bring an overall improvement in the health status of the mother and the infants. A target of extending the programme to 1,200 sub-district hospitals by the end of Seventh Plan period had been set. So far, 829 Plan Period Centres at sub-divisional hospitals have been approved. The remaining will be taken up in a phased manner. State Government have sanctioned the programme in 560 sub-divisional hospitals.

The urban revamping scheme has been introduced with a view to provide improved service delivery system of primary health care and family welfare and maternity services in urban areas. No new urban family welfare centres are to be set up, but existing urban forces are to be re-organised and new Health Posts established according to the recommendations of the working group. So far, 899 Health Posts and 14 City Family Welfare Bureaux have been reorganised. State Government have sanctioned operationalisation in 539 Health Posts and 10 City Family Welfare Bureaux.

Sterilisation beds scheme provides immediate facilities for tubectomy operations in the hospitals where such cases could not be admitted due to lack of facilities. Under the scheme, beds are sanctioned to those medical institutions and hospitals which are run by voluntary organisations on the basis of their performance during the previous year. Beds are sanctioned to the voluntary institutions on the recommendations of the State Governments and regional directors of health and family welfare of the respective States. A maintenance grant of Rs. 3,000 per bed per annum is paid to each institution, subject to the condition that a minimum of 60 tubectomise per bed per annum are performed. A total of 2,766 sterilisation beds have been approved under State Government institutions, local bodies, and voluntary organisations as on 31 March, 1986.

The Government has evolved a scheme of renovation/ remodelling IUD rooms into an operation theatre at the rural family welfare centres attached to primary health centres for providing improved facilities for sterilisation and MTP services to the population in rural areas. Primary health centres were approved on 31 March, 1986. State Governments have sanctioned the scheme in 862 PHCs as on 31 March, 1986.

Motivation and education

The family welfare programme in India depends on its voluntary acceptance by the people. To approach about 13 crore literate and illiterate couples in the reproductive age group, living in urban and remote rural areas, a broad-based mass education and motivation programme has been launched. The mass mailing unit of the Department of Family Welfare disseminates information in the form of printed materials to various categories of opinion leaders through direct mail service. Out of the list of addresses, five lakh are currently operational. In addition to this, the unit publishes two regular monthly journals—"Centre Calling" in English and "Hamara Ghar" in Hindi, and two quarterly publications—"Jan Swasth Rakshak" in Hindi and "E.P.I. Bulletin" in English. Total print orders of these periodicals are about 1.5 lakh per issue.

Area projects

Based on model plan worked out by Ministry, 67 districts of 15 States have been taken up for the intensive development of health and family welfare infrastructure and expansion of services under Area Projects with partial financial assistance of World Bank. United Nations Fund for Population Activities (UNFPA), Danish International Development Agency (DANIDA), United

States Agency for International Development (USAID), and U.K. These projects are designed to increase and strengthen, in about five years, facilities and manpower for delivery of health and family welfare services in an integrated manner to set a level that will ultimately reach the entire country over a larger period. These include information, education and communication activities including orientation training camps, mass media activities, including management training for staff, monitoring and evaluation and innovative activities. The ultimate objectives of the scheme are to reduce fertility and to reduce maternal and child mortality and morbidity.

Research and evaluation

Research activities continued in the field of demography and communication action through 18 population research centres in various States. Bio-medical research in the field of reproductive biology and fertility control is being done in the Indian Council of Medical Research, Central Drug Research Institute, All India Institute of Medical Sciences, and National Institute of Health and Family Welfare.[5]

Gap between fertility levels and fertility goals

The family welfare programme is an important national programme in the socio-economic planning of the nation. This comprehensive national programme emphasises human resource development and improving the quality of life of the people. Despite the recent progress in the implementation of the programme, the desired objectives could not be achieved so far. There is wide gap between the actual fertility levels and fertility goals laid down by the Government. Diverse social and cultural factors play an important role in the variation in acceptance and non-acceptance of the programme throughout the country. The family, the kinship structure, husband-wife decision-making, values and disvalues of children, and interpersonal communication, affect the implementation of the programme to a considerable extent.

---

5. *India—1986,* Ministry of Information and Broadcasting, Government of India, New Delhi, pp. 180-185.

Population ethics

Population ethics consists of systematic ethical reflection on population-related behaviour and population problems. Questions of ethics are present whenever population phenomena are regarded as problems and whenever population-influencing and population-responsive policies are debated. The rapid population growth is a major contributor to high unemployment, overpopulation, inadequate housing, poor sanitation, continued illiteracy, and insufficient public services.

The National Seminar on Population, Family and Culture provided a forum to participating public men, demographers, doctors, family sociologists and researchers for identifying innovative research areas on various qualitative aspects of the population programme. The country's population policy should be oriented towards developing a sound and healthysociety.

The socio-economic environment of the family

The personality of child depends much on the social and economic environment of the family for its development, as the child cannot be brought up in isolation. Some researchers have traced out that infant mortality rate and ideal family size are interrelated. Unless we can assure parents about the survivality of each live birth, we cannot ask them to restrict to two children. There is a significant correlation between socialisation of children and structure of the family. It is observed that the joint-family system ensures better health provisions for the children than the nuclear families. The inadequate distribution of nutritious diet, coupled with defective functioning of health care delivery agencies, and wide discrimination in the existing health care service distribution in the rural pockets of the country, adversely affect the maternal and child care programme at grassroot level.

The economic factors are significant in fertility decisions, both influencing the desire for large families and creating pressures to stop having children. But motivational processes are complex and economic factors do not operate independently of social and emotional considerations. The factors responsible for change in family include social legislation, urbanisation, education, industrialisation, geographical mobility, individualistic values, and contacts with Western societies. It is assumed that these factors produce inevitable change in various aspects of family structure. Although the family is the most conservative institution, only next to religion, it is not left untouched by the process of modernisation.

Chapter III

PERSONAL DATA AND FAMILY PLANNING

The Population Reference Bureau is a highly respected, non-profit, non-Government, Washington-based demographic institution. Statistics released by the Bureau in may 1990 show that India's current population is 835.035 million, compared with 816.08 million at last year's (1989) tally, showing an increase of 2.3 per cent, and that her birth rate remains at 33 per 1,000 people; but her death rate now is only 11 per 1,000, compared with 13 per 1,000 in the previous year. In other words, India's birth rate has held firm over that of last year. The already sizeable population of India is expected to double itself in only 32 years, compared with the 35-year projection made last year.[1]

The Bureau estimates that India will have a population of 1,042.5 million by the year 2000 (the 1989 projection was

1. "India's Population up by 2.3 per cent", *The Statesman*, New Delhi, 24 May, 1990, p. 9.

1,031.3 million), and 1,374.5 million in 2020 (the 1989 projection was 1,308.8 million). The infant mortality rate is down to 96 per 1,000 infants dying before their first birthday (last year's figure was 104 per 1,000), and the average Indian born today can now expect to live to be 58, compared with last year's life expectancy of 54.

India's total fertility rate (that is, the average number of children a woman will have during her child-bearing years of 15 to 49) is 4.3, the same as last year. But this is regarded as about double the 2.1 to 2.5 number of children per mother, which constitutes the "replacement level" when population stops growing. India's rate of natural increase (that is, birth rate minus death rate) remains at 2.2. In age breakdown, India's population is becoming marginally older—37 per cent are now under the age of 15 and 4 per cent over the age of 65, compared with 38 per cent and 4 per cent, respectively, last year. Family planning figures remain the same as those of last year. 40 per cent of Indian women use some form of contraceptives, but only 32 per cent among them use the more reliable modern methods of the pill, intra-uterine device, sterilisation, and other chemical or barrier methods.

The Population Reference Bureau, in its annual statistical publication, calls the 1990s a crucial decade for world population stabilisation. It reports that the world gained nearly a quarter billion people since it passed the 5-billion mark two years ago. The current total is 5.234 billion, and now the Bureau predicts that the 6-billion mark will be reached in 10 years.

Birth rates have dropped in some countries such as Thailand, China, and Indonesia, but there is little evidence of change in others. As life expectancy improves, death rates go down and, without a decrease in birth rate, the population grows faster. While world population growth rates slowed during the 1970s, they re-accelerated during the 1980s. The world population growth now increases at a rate of 1.8 per cent. (India's growth rate is much higher—2.3 per cent). Curiously, Italy—the homeland of the Catholic Church and its precepts against birth control—now boasts the lowest fertility rate (1.2 lifetime births per woman).

Also, the developing nations, with the highest growth rates, now account for 77 per cent of the global population and are expected to reach 84 per cent by the year 2020. Life expectancy is the lowest in Chad (39 years) and Sierre Leone (40 years), and the highest in Iceland and Japan (78 years). In USA, the average baby born today is expected to live to be 75.

India is behind China in national population. China's population now is reported to be 1,103.9 million (compared with 1,087 million last year), with estimates that she will reach 1.291.6 million by the year 2000, and 1,523.2 million by the year 2020. But China's birth rate is only 21 per 1,000 (compared with India's 33), and her death rate is 7 per 1,000 (compared with India's 11). China's net growth rate now is 1.4 per cent, well below the global average, and her total fertility rate of children per woman is 2.4, just a little more than half of India's.

The Population Reference Bureau ranks the world's 10 most populous countries as China (1,103.9 million), India (853.035 million), the Soviet Union (288.7 million), USA (248.8 million), Indonesia (184.6 million), Brazil (147.4 million), Japan (123.2 million), Nigeria (115.3 million), Bangladesh (114.7 million), and Pakistan (110.4 million). By the year 2020, Nigeria is projected to move up to the sixth place, and Pakistan to the seventh. Japan, because of her stabilised population, is expected to drop to eleventh position, and Mexico to move up to the tenth position.

The idea of controlling births in India was mooted over 60 years ago, when the growth of population was not perceived as directly related to the economic development of the country, and when the pressure of population was not as palpable as it is today. The magnitude of the problem and the urgency it demands necessitate a fresh re-thinking on the methods and measures to overcome it. We shall have to adopt all measures we may lay our hands on, consistent with ethical and philosophical scruples, before it is too late, before we reach a point of no-return, as some demographers and social scientists put it.

Today, rapid rates of population growth are leading to rapid increase in the numbers of the ill-fed, ill-clad, and ill-housed. should death-rates, then, rise again to cut back the increasing numbers? None of the awakened people would admit this as a sane solution. Yet it is obvious to all that growing science and technology will permit an adequate life-span to the people who live now and who may live at the end of the present and the beginning of the next century. What, then, is the solution?

The most critical aspect of the population problem is that of timing. Rapid population growth would not have been a major problem, if it had occurred along with rapid economic and social development. If the major problem is the achievement of rapid economic growth, the major hazard is rapid population growth. A major aspect of development planning is, therefore, the slowing down of population growth. If so, small families should be equated with nutrition, health, and education as individual and social goals.

Recent population figures are mind-boggling. The major emphasis has, therefore, been placed on the family planning programme launched by the Central and State Governments. What is depressing is that, in spite of huge allocation of money to family planning programmes in no less than seven five-year plans, there has been little appreciable fall in the birth-rate. If the family planning programme is to be successful, the undertaking of extensive and intensive analysis of motivating factors underlying the adoption of family planning by our people is necessary

Sex ratio

The pressures exerted by excessive population growth have a deep impact on all members of the society in different ways—not only through shortages of material necessities and amenities but also through a dangerous lowering of quality in human resource development (for example in educational standards).

What, however, is still not being fully appreciated is the fact that the stultifying effects created by this situation will impinge most cruelly on the growing generation, on whom depends the future of society. In other words, present-day parents who, due to whatever circumstances, heedlessly continue to have large families are doing a great disservice to their own progeny who, in turn, might deepen the crisis by again repeating the pattern when they themselves become parents, unless they arrive at a full realisation of the truth in good time.

For these reasons, it is desirable that one of the spouses gets himself or herself sterilised after one child or two children according to the norm they wish to adopt. It may be added that vasectomy (VT for men) is easier and quicker than tubectomy (TT for women), though both are 100 per cent efficient and produce no side-effects.

Table 15 sums up the date on the sex ratio between the respondents in the sample.

Table 15

HOSHANGABAD SLUMS : SEX RATIO

Sex	*Respondents*	*Percentage*	*Ranking*
Men	142	47.3	2
Women	158	52.7	1
Total	300	100	—

Source : Personal Investigation.

The table discloses the majority of 52.7 per cent women and a substantial proportion of 47.3 per cent men. If the 1.7 per cent of the widows, 3.7 per cent of the divorced, and 2.6 per cent of separated (8 per cent in all), vide Table 17. were already conversant with the implications of the population problem and the desirability of the small-family norm, they must have been in a better position to discover the methods and plan to have a small family right form the beginning. To start educating parents about the small-family norm when they are already deep set in their ways (and probably have three or four children), is rather like starting to dig a well when fire is consuming the house.

Age-group

We believe that the objective of family planning is the enrichment of human life, not its restriction, and that family planning, by assuring greater opportunity to each person, frees man to attain his individual dignity and reach his full potential. There are important links between population growth and the implementation of the rights and freedoms proclaimed in the Universal Declaration of Human Rights. Population planning is not only an integral part of society's efforts for economic and social development but is also a way to human progress in modern society. Man has shown increasing ability to master his environment. He is now acquiring the knowledge as well as the means to master himself and his own future. It is his duty to do so for his own sake and for the sake of succeeding generations to whom he must bequeath a life worthy of human beings.

For these and other reasons, it was necessary that we should identify our respondents according to their age-groups before proceeding with our investigation. The period between 16 years and 30 years in one's life, in general, is a period of the greatest reproductivity, while the age-period between 31 years and 40 years is one when the children born in the preceding age-period should be in school or college, in service or self-employment. Our thinking is that, in order to stick to the small-family norm, and to ensure the health and happiness of the mother as well as to reduce the cares and anxieties of the father, couples should take care that no child is born when they attain the age of 35.

Table 16 indicates the data on the age-groups of individuals whose responses to the family welfare programmes in the slum areas of Hoshangabad are under study.

Table 16
Hoshangabad Slums : Age-group

Age-group	*Respondents*	*Percentage*	*Ranking*
Between 16 and 20 years	74	24.7	2
Between 21 and 25 years	122	40.7	1
Between 26 and 30 years	56	18.7	3
Between 31 and 40 years	43	14.3	4
Over 40 years	5	1.6	5
Total	300	100	—

Source : Personal Investigation.

The table shows that the majority of 40.7 per cent respondents were in the age-group of 21-25 years, followed by 24.7 per cent respondents who were in the age-group of 16-20 years. The latter age-group suggests that early marriage is also prevalent among the slum-dwellers of Hoshangabad, specially the marriage of teen-age girls. In other words, the couples between the age of 16 and 20 were clamped into a domestic routine, with children to bring up, before they themselves had matured in terms of worldly experience. Had they belonged to a better social strata, these boys and girls would have been studying in various educational institutions. While 18.7 per cent respondents were between 26 and 30 years, the lesser number of 14.3 per cent respondents were in the 31-40 age-group. The minority of 1.6 per cent respondents, in our sample survey, were above 40 years.

Marital status

Family planning is no doubt urgently needed to help in attaining adequate levels of food, shelter, clothing, employment, education, health, recreation, and other basic material amenities for all members of society. It is also urgently needed to reach higher levels of living where the human spirit can unfold itself, instead of being degraded or destroyed with its poverty levels, both physically and mentally.

Ascertaining the marital status of individuals is, therefore, important in order to study how they respond towards family planning programmes in Hoshangabad slums. If they are married, we come to know what role they have played—whether successfully, perfunctorily, or unsuccessfully—in planning as well as health management of their family. If they are married, interpersonal contact with them helps us in eliciting information whether they have any plans with regard to the size and welfare of the family they will bring up. If one of the spouses has predeceased the other, or is divorced or separated, but still young and hoping to remarry, interviewing such respondent has a double advantage : we learn from the interviewees what he or she had done with regard to planned parenthood and family health during the first marriage, and what he or she has in mind with regard to this crucial demand of modern existence if he or she marries again.

Table 17

Hoshangabad Slums : Marital Status

Marital Status	*Respondents*	*Percentage*	*Ranking*
Married	276	92.0	1
Unmarried	—	—	—
Widow/Widower	5	1.7	4
Divorced	11	3.7	2
Separated	8	2.6	3
Total	300	100	—

Source : Personal Investigation.

The table reveals thatnoneoftherespondents in the sample was unmarried. The vast majority of 92 per cent respondents were married. The minority of 3.7 per cent respondents were divorced. Another minority of 2.6 per cent respondents were separated, while an almost negligible proportion of 1.7 among the slum-dwellers consisted of either widows or widowers.

These five groups of respondents offer a rich field for examining the success or otherwise of the population policy and family planning programmes in the slum areas of Hoshangabad, which is interlocked with a reorientation of values, attitudes and behaviour patterns, taking into account the realities of present-day life, efforts to modernise and to move towards the 21st century which is fast approaching.

Educational status

Education, in all its manifold forms, is the instrument by which society transforms itself from what it is into what it hopes to be. In a sense, we may regard education as cultural growth. Occupational mobility is achieved through education, but when the school differentiates students early in their educational career, it denies to those who are allotted inferior status the only opportunity they have for social mobility.

There is a definite correlation between the educational attainment of women and the number of children they tend to have. Raising the age of marriage is undoubtedly a much-needed reform, with the necessary changes in the social climate. This is needed not only from the viewpoint of planning families but also for its own sake. It would also yield other beneficial results : it would help in raising the status of women through better opportunities for education, employment, and the development of personality.

In general, the higher and wider the level of one's education, the more the skill to understand things in their proper perspective. Theoretically, exceptions, apart, an individual educated up to the primary level tends to have a better perception than one who is illiterate. Similarly, an individual schooled up to the higher secondary level is likely to be more responsive to the socio-economic stimuli around him than one with only primary education. This responsiveness to the changing situation, with which an individual is perpetually besieged, goes on increasing with each step upward in the educational ladder, and even throughout life.

Table 18 registers data on the educational level of respondents inhabiting Hoshangabad slums.

Table 18

HOSHANGABAD SLUMS : EDUCATIONAL STATUS

Educational status	*Respondents*	*Percentage*	*Ranking*
Illiterate	226	75.3	1
Literate	29	9.7	2
Primary (Class V)	21	7.0	3
Middle (Class VIII)	13	4.3	4
Higher Secondary (Class XI)	11	3.7	5
Total	300	100	—

Source : Personal Investigation.

The table reveals that the vast majority of 75.3 per cent respondents living in the 9 slums of Hoshangabad are illiterate, which seems to be a general characteristic of the slum population not only in Madhya Pradesh but also all over India. The remaining 24.7 per cent of the respondents are unequally distributed in terms of educational levels. 9.3 per cent of them are literate, perhaps because of the adult literacy drive. By "literate", we mean an individual who knows simple reading and writing but who head no formal education up to the primary level.

7 per cent of the slum respondents are educated up to the primary level, that is, they have passed Class V. 4.3 per cent have read up to the middle school level, having passed Class VIII. 3.7 per cent respondents had their schooling up to the higher secondary level, that is, they had passed Class XI. As the level of education rises, the proportion of respondents decreases, because of drop-outs largely caused by economic necessity.

Occupational status

The population of the nine slums of Hoshangabad falls under four broad categories—employees, petty traders, agriculturists, and unemployed. The employed slum-dwellers are more in Class IV than in class III jobs, while some are self-employed working as washermen, barbers, potters, carpenters, fishermen, milkmen, and casual labourers. Respondents engaged in petty business are vegetable-sellers, fish-sellers, petty hawkers, and tea-vendors. Some of them sell their commodities in *thelas* or push-carts, moving from one locality to another. A few of them have turned the front portion of their shanties into petty shops, selling a few items of grocery and also cheap wares.

The agricultural group includes those handful who own a couple of acres of land, but the majority of them are landless agricultural labourers who take up non-agricultural work to earn their livelihood during the off-season. The others were temporarily unemployed when the data was collected.

Table 19 delineates the occupational status of the slum-dwellers in our sample survey.

Table 19

Hoshangabad Slums : Occupational Status

Occupational status	*Respondents*	*Percentage*	*Ranking*
Employment	29	9.7	4
Business	181	60.3	1
Agriculture	58	19.3	2
Unemployed	32	10.7	3
Total	300	100	—

Source : Personal Investigation.

The table discloses that the minority of 9.7 per cent slum-residents are able to get jobs as petty employees or are self-employed doing less remunerative work, while 10.7 per cent are currently out of work. The largest proportion of the slum-dwellers earn their daily bread through petty business, working largely as hawkers and pedlars, selling perishable agricultural commodities like vegetables, fruits, fish, eggs, and sometimes trinkets and cheap ornamental articles.

The next largest proportion of 19.3 per cent slum-residents are engaged in agricultural activities—preparing the field, sowing, watering, weeding, harvesting, bundling, threshing, winnowing, packing, and the like. Many of them are low-paid wage-earners.

A few have inherited little plots of land, from which they eke out a living. A few others keep one or two buffaloes and sell milk, or poultry and sell chicken and eggs.

These facts and figures indicate that the slum population of Hoshangabad does not belong to the "privileged" section society. Being largely illiterate or just literate, the slum people are unable to climb up the social ladder. Their very residence in slums suggests that, in general, they belong to the weaker section of society—weaker economically, socially, and educationally—denied the good things of life, and struggling hard to make both ends meet. It is just for these reasons that they should attract the attention of family planning workers the most. In fact, they deserve first priority in all family planning and family welfare programmes.

Family planning in slums

It is the need of the hour that the family planning movement should become the people's revolution. Evidently, people would need to be motivated to a level where they would themselves seek out family planning services. The amount of work done in past years leads one to believe that the family planning programme in Madhya Pradesh is well on the way of becoming the people's revolution, for which it is essential to intensify family planning services not only in urban slums but also in remote rural areas. The policy at present is to lay equal emphasis on both terminal and non-terminal methods of family planning, but it may become necessary to shift the emphasis to non-terminal methods in future to achieve the objectives of the programme.

Expressed in simple terms, a doubling of population has occurred since independence. Many reasons are attributed to the slow decline in the birth rate. Improvement in nutritional levels, rising standards of living, and urbanisation trends are believed to influence fertility declined. But age at marriage and literacy—especially female literacy—are considered to be the two most important contributors to fertility decline.

Postponement of marriage by women can have a greater impact on population growth. An educational process should also highlight the ill effects of early marriage. The need to educate our people regarding the disastrous effects of early marriages among the illiterate, specially in urban slums and rural areas, requires coordinated efforts by the public health, education, and tribal welfare departments. A strong link with the social welfare departments is also necessary, because programmes of adult literacy and improving the nutritional intake of women and children can be utilised to persuade women to adopt the small-family norm. Coordination among all these departments is essential to convert the family planning movement into the people's revolution.

Family planning is not a total failure in India. Yet there is an urgent need for fresh thinking on the family planning programme strategy. The programme should be viewed as a revolution leading to social change. The aim should be to bring about a change in the traditional values. The family planning programme should not be considered as a medical programme alone. There is need for creating social consciousness so that young men and women consider it a duty, in their own interest as well as in the interest of the society of which they are an integral part, to marry late and to have fewer children.

In this sense, family planning is an essential part of the strategy of enlarging welfare. In fact, greater social and economic welfare is the only reason for family planning. We need such welfare, not because we are against children, but because we want every child to have the best opportunity possible in life.

Population limitation, thus, becomes inevitable, not only for survival, but also for the quality of survival. There is no workable alternative to family planning. It is the gap between fertility rates and mortality rates that determines population growth. The concept of a large family, which was a common feature in India, is no longer tenable. Social change is a slow process, but the large content of socially backward and economically weaker sections in urban slums and rural areas makes the task more difficult and the pace of progress is rendered slower.

Role of the family planning worker in slum areas

Family planning has functional aspects also. It is increasingly realised that family planning is really a social problem, which requires indispensable help from medical men. For this reason, the role of the family planning workers in slum areas makes it essential that he should have certain skills and dynamism. It is the primary responsibility of the family planning worker to know the residents of the slum well. He should study their socio-economic conditions and their reasons for resistance. He should influence the minds of the slum-dwellers, so that they may move in the desired direction. The success of the family planning worker depends on how best he can motivate the slum-residents to accept family planning methods.

The role of the family planning worker should no more be limited to the distribution of contraceptives in slum areas or the health centre. He should act as a helper-educator and be quick in changing the attitude of the slum population. He has to make the slum people, especially the women, family planning-minded in order that they may have access to scientific advice regarding sex problems, psychological disorders, and techniques of contraception.

The programme of family planning can bring more fruitful results in slum areas, if the medium of interpersonal approach is adopted to create pressure on the reproductive behaviour along with the combination of birth control. The family planning worker can very well be the medium of interpersonal approach. He needs to be well acquainted with the cultural background of the people living in slums among whom he has to work. A thorough insight into the cultural fabric of the "subject" alone can make him understand the real force which governs the acceptance or rejection of family planning techniques. This knowledge, combined with the proper orientation for approaching in the right manner, can help him in achieving his desired goals.

The special professionally trained family planning worker can mould tradition views by explaining the role and importance of children. He can be of great help in changing the attitude of the slum people regarding modern contraceptive devices. He is aware that what is needed are short-cuts to the wider cumulative social change which will help in creating new pressures on reproductive behaviour. The change in the attitude of the slum people is a gradual process which needs planned and conscious efforts. The services of a trained worker play a major role in family planning, and his contribution is the very essence of such planning.

Chapter IV

FAMILY DATA AND FAMILY PLANNING

The major problem in the country today is the problem of poverty, and every other scheme or activity gains significance only in so far as it helps us to deal with this central issue. It is quite clear that poverty is the main cause for the massive increase in our population, because the rate of population growth shows a sharp decline whenever living standards of people begin to rise. It does not mean that over-population is the main cause of our poverty. The optimum size of population depends on a number of production factors and the status of modern technology.

Poverty is the cause of high population or vice versa. It will be more useful to concentrate upon trying to see what specifically can be done in the organised sector to extend education regarding family planning among the working classes, and to provide increasing facilities to help them limit the size of their families in their own interest.

It is no longer possible to look upon family planning as a programme standing in isolation. It has to be integrated into the entire complex of health and nutrition programmes, and must teach the individuals about its importance and necessity. Family planning, as mentioned earlier, must be transformed from a programme of the Government of India into a genuine mass movement. For this purpose, an entirely new motivational strategy will have to be worked out, in which individual monetary incentives are kept to the minimum necessary to cover loss of wages, and the educational aspects of the programme highlighted in a manner which will make it truly relevant to the masses. State Governments and local bodies down to and including the panchayats, voluntary organizations, as well as the organised sector, will all have to be involved in a massive effort if real success has to be achieved.

The position of women in society is absolutely central to any programme of family planning. Apart from the guarantees in our constitution, a whole spectrum of social, educational and legal measures need to be taken to ensure that women in fact do enjoy an equal position in all spheres of national life including the family. The interest of working women will have to be fully safeguarded.[1]

Almost every pregnancy is a natural corollary of the married state, and for the most part pregnancies are accidents, and not products of design. Babies arrive by chance, and not by choice. for a pregnancy to occur under ideal conditions, the wife should first undergo a general medical examination to decide whether she is fit to become a mother. Such fitness can be considered from several points of view, namely, primarily, (a) physical, emotional and mental health; and, secondarily, (b) economic and social conditions. A large number of pregnancies that occur are undesirable in the sense that they are ill-advised from the point-of view of the mother's health. The mother may be anaemic or weak, may suffer from some reproductive disorder or deformity,

---

1. Singh, Karan, *Population, Poverty and the Future of India*, National Institute of Family Planning, 1975, pp. 23-26.

or may have too large a family already to have enough energy and leisure to cope with another baby; and, lastly, the strain on the slender family purse may be considerable.

The problems are the absence of limitation of family size and lack of spacing of children. If every pregnancy could occur under conditions that satisfy all the relevant factors, the infant mortality rate could be reduced to a very low and nominal figure. If family planning were practised by every couple, this end could be much more easily achieved. If children can be spaced for three years apart, the mother can cope with the children and their demands. Family planning must become efficient enough to limit the number of children to two or three at the most, under present-day circumstances of poverty and unemployment. This would put an end to present improvident maternity, and lower not only infant morality but also maternal mortality. Infant mortality is greater among families of improvident births where children arrive too often and too close to one another.

All maternal and child health institutions distribute conventional contraceptives. All maternity hospitals offer sterilization and intrauterine contraceptive device insertion services. In the daily routine in the clinic and home visits, maternal and child health personnel render follow-up services to couples who are practising family planning and discuss about family planning with those who are yet not doing so. They also motivate couples to adopt a suitable method for planning their children and offer the necessary services for the purpose. In the antenatal period, the mothers are told about puerperal sterilization. If they wish to adopt the method, delivery is arranged in a hospital and a tubectomy performed. For others, the subject is discussed in the post-natal period and the required contraceptives are given. With this integration, family planning has been given a new slant. Family planning does not merely mean limitation of the family or spacing of children, but it also implies taking adequate care of the health of the family and more care towards the living children. It is realised that couples are much more likely to practise contraception if they are guaranteed that the children they already have will be looked after and their proper health care ensured to enable them to survive the health problems and accidents of early life.

The maternal and child health (MCH) centres and family planning clinics attend to immunization and nutritional programmes also. Mothers who come along with their children to the clinics or to the centres, are attended to and given the necessary child health services.

Antenatal care in general has two objectives : (i) to conserve the health of the expectant mother in pregnancy, labour and during the laying-in period, and (ii) to enable the mother to produce a healthy child with the highest possible potentiality of developing into a healthy adult.

In the words of a British study on the general problems of maternity : "The aim of the antenatal movement is to make contact with each expectant mother as early as possible in pregnancy and keep her under regular supervision, viz., monthly during the first four months, then fortnightly until the eighth month, and thereafter weekly until confinement.[2]

Certain specific services are designed to remove the fear and anxiety of the expectant mother, especially when she is a primigravida, to diagnose and treat any early complications, to increase the proportions of normal deliveries, to lower the maternity, morbidity and mortality rates, and, lastly, to reduce the incidence of premature births, still-births, perinatal and neo-natal deaths.

Prematurity and immaturity are outstanding causes of infant mortality in the neo-natal period. The state of health of mother during pregnancy, her economic, social and nutritional condition play a important part in the incidence of premature births.

To lessen the incidence of premature births, certain measures can be taken. In order to allow every expectant mother the

---

2. *Maternity in Great Britain,* Oxford University Press, London, 1978, p. 29.

benefit of pre-natal care, a large number of pre-natal clinics are necessary. These clinics should be situated at proper distance to serve certain areas and be easily accessible to all.

The clinics and health centres should be staffed by medical women and a sufficient number of health visitors, to allow for the follow-up and education of every expectant mother attending the clinic. Proper laboratory facilities should exist for all pathological examinations, so as to allow for early diagnosis and treatment of complications.

Besides the medical care available, which should include giving of liver and/or iron according to the blood report, amenities in the way of milk and additional nutrition to supplement what is lacking in the home diet should be arranged for at the clinic. Every mother should be made to realise the importance and advantages of early and sustained pre-natal care for herself and her unborn child. A sufficient number of pre-natal beds should be provided in maternity hospitals to allow for observation and treatment of complications which threaten premature labour.

Improvement in the economic status of the expectant mother is very necessary. Her standard of living should be raised, her housing conditions improved, and diets so constituted as to be balanced. The diet should include the required amount of protective foods and provide sufficient caloric value.

Some measures should be taken to lower the incidence of deaths in premature infants. Intra-natal care can be obtained during labour of a skilled obstetrician, an expert physician, a paediatrician, and specialized nursing facilities required to aid the survival of the newly-born premature and immature infants. Reduction of neo-natal mortality can only be effected by expert and trained care during the early neo-natal period. In the majority of mothers, this can only be possible by hospitalisation, where such care would be available. Delivery in the house would allow the infant very little chance of survival, for, in addition to unsuitable home conditions, there is lack of intelligent care from the mother or relatives.

The maternity institutions should arrange to have separate staff of nurses, specially trained in the care and management of the premature infant, so as to be at hand for every premature birth. A separate premature baby ward, away from the general lying-in ward, suitably equipped and heated for the isolation and care of the pre-mature infants, is also necessary. It can be judged that neo-natal mortality is the chief factor responsible for swelling the infant mortality rate and that it is entirely preventible.

It is important that every expectant mother should receive expert care during the entire period of pregnancy so as to safeguard her and her infant and help to save many previous lives. Expectant mothers are encouraged to register as early as possible at the weekly or biweekly ante-natal clinic organised by the different agencies. The clinics carry routine health check-ups and specialized examinations, if necessary, and give health and nutrition education. The needs are simple, but not easy to meet. Expectant mothers should be medically examined and in normal cases home delivery by a trained midwife arranged for. If there are any complications, the mother-to-be must be referred to a hospital where necessary arrangements for confinement with competent obstetrical care can be made.

It is physically impossible for the midwife or nurse-midwife to provide skilled assistance in all normal births, especially now that they have become multipurpose workers. If pre-natal care is important, post-natal care is equally important. Post-natal care, unlike ante-natal case, involves not only the mother's own health but also the infant's and the mother's ability to take care of the infant.

Post-natal clinics are organised only in the teaching hospitals and larger maternity hospitals. Mostly, post-natal clinics are combined with child welfare clinics. But the attendance of mothers is not satisfactory. They do not report back to clinics unless they experience major illness. Maternal and child health field personnel give pre-natal health supervision to the extent possible during visits.

The foremost requisite is that the Government and the community set up infant welfare centres where mothers can receive advice, assurance, and some instruction to protect the infant from neo-natal infection due to poor sanitary and hygienic environment. The mother also needs to be taught antiseptic routine to guard the infant from familiar infections.

This stage of infant development in that of feeding. In all cultures, breast-breeding is natural and preferred to artificial feeding, so long as the mother's milk has not dried up for health or psychological reasons. If the infant can obtain the necessary amount of nutrition through the mother's milk, half the battle is won. Mother's milk at the early stages need not be supplemented and the question of cleanliness and purity does not arise. Should the mother's milk fail, or should the mother be unable to breast-feed adequately for any other reason, bottle-feeding has to be resorted to. Sterilization, or even careful washing with soap and hot water of bottles, is not an accepted procedure in most homes. The reason is one of ignorance and poverty—ignorance of the need for cleanliness, and poverty which renders and purchase of the necessary equipment for artificial feeding beyond the power of the mother and her family.

Maternal and child health personnel either vaccinate infants themselves or get it done by the sanitary inspectors and basic health workers. Mothers need to be taught about infant care. Knowledge about bearing and rearing children is derived from a fund of folklore, traditionally handed down from mother to daughter. While there is no doubt that the folklore contains profound knowledge and robust commonsense based on centuries of human experience, there are areas where this knowledge is at glaring variance with the scientific verdict. These areas include infant feeding, clothing, and treatment of common ailments. At present, the need is to educate every mother in the latest scientific findings and in the most desirable methods for rearing the infants to ensure their proper physical emotional development. It is the mother and the home that are more important than all the infant welfare institutions, and the medical personnel.

Sir James and others in their survey of *A Thousand Families in New Castle upon Tyne* writes :

> "In the study of these families and in attempting to correlate their environments with the health of the children, there emerged one dominating factor, the capacity of the mother. If she failed, her children suffered. If she coped with life skilfully and pluckily, she was a safeguard of their health. In spite of lapses and failures the mother stands out as the cornerstone of the family structure, and other experience confirms that in all sections of society she remains the chief guardian of child welfare, a fact which is sometimes in danger of being forgotten. A family with a good mother can withstand a reckless or even a vicious father but rarely can a family survive if the mother fails."[3]

It is difficult to define this "capacity of the mothers". Any attempt at definition can be more negative than positive. At one end, we have stupid ignorant and incapable mothers, some of whom are emotionally unfit to be mothers at all, and at the other end there are mothers who organise and run a home and bring up children with care, love and wisdom. The entire credit goes to the mother where sickness is rare and infant mortality absent. The role of the mother is an important role in ensuring a happy and healthy family. The main point is that "maternal capacity" is neither instinctive nor hereditary. It is largely teachable.

The problem is made more complicated by the low level of nutrition and environmental sanitation of the community. It has been estimated that almost half of the admissions in children's hospitals are infants. The child health organisation and maternal care finds that, in spite of the fact that problems of early childhood demand prompt care, it is the most difficult group to reach. It is seen that the children are brought to the child welfare clinics

---

3. James Spence, et al. *A Thousand Families in New Castle upon Tyne,* University Press, London, p. 120.

only when they are is need of urgent care. Much has to be done to educate mothers in the act of child and mother-craft.

Family planning finds its place in the society as a programme of the highest priority. Its importance is reflected in the widespread public interest no less than in the magnitude of the effort, organisation, and finance which Government is devoting to the programme.

Previously, family planning was not integrated with maternity and child care, but now this has to be done if the family planning is to be made more effective. Family welfare planning centres include the scheme of immunization of infants and pre-school children with D.P.T (Diphtheria, Polio, Tetanus) immunization of expectant mothers against tetanus, prophylaxis against nutritional anaemia for mothers and children, and a nutritional programme for control of blindness caused by Vitamin A deficiency among children. Family planning will be effectively integrated with general health services of primary health centres and sub-centres.

It is a poor policy to neglect mothers and the infants who are the future citizens of our country. Human resources constitute the most powerful factor in the prosperity of a nation. Both the health and character of a nation depend upon its mothers who give birth to the future citizens of our country. The welfare of the society, truly speaking, depends on the attention and care bestowed on the most defenceless and vulnerable section of our population—the mother and her infant.

Members in the family

With the average monthly income of a slum family, accompanied by mounting inflation throughout the country, it is self-explanatory that a large-size family is comparatively in a tighter situation than a small-size family as regards the basic necessities of life, not to speak of comforts, while luxury is something beyond the dreams of slum-dwellers. The economic, educational, and social backwardness of slum-dwellers, rare exceptions apart, serve almost as strong barriers in climbing up the economic, educational, and social ladder.

Economic backwardness denies the slum residents many good things of life. Educational backwardness makes them prisoners of ignorance and superstition. Social backwardness stands in the way of social equality and ends up in social discrimination. All these factors, combined together, affect their psyche adversely, breeding in them sterility of ambition, an attitude of defeatism and fatalism and a sense of resignation of their inevitable lot.

Table 20 delineates data on the number of members the slum families under survey have.

Table 20

Hoshangabad Slums : Members in the Family

Family members	*Respondents*	*Percentage*	*Ranking*
4 members	92	30.7	2
5 members	149	49.7	1
6 members	59	19.6	3
Total	300	100	—

Source : Personal Investigation.

The table reveals that the largest proportion of 49.7 per cent slum families have 5 members each, all living together under the same roof. The next largest proportion of 30.7 per cent families have 4 members each which, in general, suggests parents and two children when the survey was undertaken. The minority of 19.6 per cent families have 6 members each, which denotes not only overcrowding and absence of privacy in their small residential space but also economic difficulties. The widowed, the divorced, and the separated have a relatively harder time, irrespective of the fact whether their family have less or more members.

Siblings living with the family

It is indeed unfortunate that, in addition to the married couple and their children, the slum family should be encumbered with some relatives, many of them being non-earning ones. They have no other place to go to and are under compulsion to seek the protection and hospitality, however feeble and grudging, of the slum family to which they happen to be related. Such relatives, are brothers and sisters bound to the family by ties of natural love and affection. The others are father-in-law and mother-in-law, many of them quite elderly and incapable of earning a regular income. Still others are the unmarried sister/sisters-in-law and brother/brothers-in-law who, if not being wage-earners, are expected to do household work to earn their keep.

Table 21 lists the number of siblings living with the slum family.

Table 21
HOSHANGABAD SLUMS : SIBLINGS LIVING WITH THE FAMILY

Relationship	*Families*	*Number of siblings*	*Ranking*
Brother(s)	3	4	6
Sister(s)	4	6	5
Father-in-law	8	8	3
Mother-in-law	10	10	1
Sister(s)-in-law	9	10	2
Brother(s)-in-law	5	7	4
Total	39	45	—
None	261	—	—

Source : Personal Investigation.

The table discloses that, among the 300 slum families surveyed, 261 or 87 per cent families had no siblings living with them. The remaining 39 families were burdened with 45 siblings, which works out to an average of 1.15 siblings per family. The next largest number of 9 families had 10 sister/sisters-in-law living with them, followed by 8 families where the father-in-law resided with them, and then followed by 5 families with brother/brothers-in-law. The least number is that of 3 families which included 4 brothers in all. These statistics show that, owing to their being largely weaker sections of society, only 13 per cent of the slum families in the sample survey are able to keep one or two relatives with them, and not more. The concept of a large joint family therefore cannot be entertained by them on account of economic and housing constraints.

Literacy/education of parents and grandparents

Social change in terms of literacy/education of grandparents and parents can be statistically measured by the increase between the literacy/education of the two generations: increase showing favourable change, and decrease revealing unfavourable change. As literacy/education of parents has some impact on children, literate/educated parents would also like their children to be literate/educated atleast up to, if not higher than, the level of literacy/education than they themselves had achieved, which suggests a movement forward. Illiterates who encourage their children to have some formal education also move in the forward direction. Illiterates who keep their children illiterate like themselves reveal a level of stagnation. Those literates or educated who deny the new educational facilities to their children take a step backwards : they are educationally retrogressive.

Table 22 provides data on the literacy/education of parents and grandparents of respondent in Hoshangabad slums.

Table 22
LITERACY/EDUCATION OF PARENTS AND GRANDPARENTS

Literacy/education	*Respondents*	*Ranking*
Father's	36	1
Mother's	8	2
Total	44	—
Husband's	57	1
Wife's	17	2
Total	74	—

Source : Personal Investigation.

Vide Table 18, out of 300 respondents, 226 or 75.3 per cent were illiterate, while the remaining 74 or 24.7 per cent were literate/educated. The present table reveals that there was more literacy among husbands (57 or 19 per cent husbands) than among wives (17 or 6.7 per cent wives). Similarly, among grandparents, a total of only 44 individuals were literate/educated: the ratio being 36 : 8, that is, 36 grandfathers and only 8 grandmothers. The figures reveal a rise in literacy/education in the sample survey: an increase of 30 individuals or 10 per cent (74 literate/educated parents as against only 44 literate/educated grandparents). The highest increase has been in women's literacy/education, which has slightly doubled (17 mothers as against only 8 grandmothers).

Summing Up

The fundamental biological obligation of the married couples should be that they should limit their family size to two or three children, with proper spacing of these children, and not producing, under any circumstances, unwanted children. The fourth child must be considered an unwanted child.

Many children are born due to some religious taboos: for example, in Hindu religion a son is a "must" to continue their generation. Such compulsions should be removed and children are not to be produced in response to political demands, religious injunctions, or cultural compulsions. "No couple need assume that the small-family norm is applicable only to the poor and the under privileged, and that they are exempt by virtue of intellectual superiority wealth, or physical stamina. Those couples determined to have more than two or three children should adopt homeless children who are already there in this world."[4]

4. Chandrasekhar, S., *Infant Mortality, Population, and Family Planning in India*, 1942, p. 323.

Chapter V

ECONOMIC DATA AND FAMILY PLANNING

With control of fertility as an immediate necessity, the family planning programmes are to be pursued vigorously. In this process, there is a need to reconcile two possibly conflicting facts of the family planning endeavour—the national good and the interest of the individual. These may often run at cross purposes to the serious detriment of the programme. Much cannot be achieved by coercion, though theoretically it is a possibility. Hence the only other alternative is guided persuasion which, in course of time, with economic development and the concomitant efforts, will culminate in the ideal of every motivated couple going after some method or the other of family planning and willing to pay for it.

With such a large population-base, communication is a real barrier which requires concentrated attention. The limitations of a programme of the nature of family planning arise not from finance but essentially from considerations of organisation and personnel which affect the scale and intensity with which the programme can be implemented. The recent development in the country to integrate the family planning with maternity and child welfare programmes are in the right direction, though much is yet to be done.

Recent thinking on the subject is that voluntary organisations could do a lot in regard to motivations of the public. Coercion will not be successful unless it has the backing of the community, and for creating such a backing the conscience of the community has to be aroused. This can best be undertaken by the third force, the volunteers in community service. It is encouraging to note that Government has realised this and is making efforts to involve voluntary organisations more and more in family planning work. Even if we are able to bring together the resources in the best possible mix, success would lie only in how best and how soon we could waken the individual motivation towards the common goal.

The world's population, including India's, continues to increase at an alarming rate. In 1985 alone, 80 million people were added to the total world population—as much as the population of Britain and Canada combined. The rapid population increase poses a serious threat to development efforts of the less developed countries. The task of providing food, schools, employment, health facilities, housing, and other amenities for the increasing number is staggering. The population question is not merely quantitative but also qualitative in nature, as the implications of population growth upon the quality of life and the well-being of the people are vitally important.

The World Commission of Environment and Development noted that people alone are not the problem. In fact, the question is one of access to resources and the ways people are able to use them. Properly treated, the earth's resources can be used more effectively and efficiently, while ensuring that they are still around to serve the next generation. Achieving this will not be easy. Development is inextricably intertwined with improvements in health, education, and the quality of life. These, in turn, are directly affected by the environment.

A crucial area of concern is the role of women. Fertility rates fall as women's employment opportunities outside the home and farm, their access to education, and their age at marriage, all rise. Broader education can have a widespread effect. Improved health, lower fertility, and better nutrition will depend on greater literacy and social and civic responsibility. Education can induce all these, and can enhance a society's ability to overcome poverty, increase incomes, improve health and nutrition, and reduce family size.

In recent years, there has been a growing concern about the widening gap between population growth and food supply in developing countries, in view of rapid population growth. Available food supplies are inadequate in nutritive quantity for a healthy and active life. Retarded development and poor health are responsible for low stamina and low physical activity. Low physical activity results in low productivity which, in turn, causes more poverty and more inadequate food supply. Unless this vicious circle is broken, the future generation will have a lower level of physical capacity and consequently reduced working efficiency.

It has been estimated by the United Nation's Food and Agriculture Organisation that in order to provide sufficient food for the vulnerable groups of the population, the total food supply in the developing countries will have to be increased by 75 per cent during the period 1965-80 and by 225 per cent during the period 1965-2000.[1] This implies an annual rate of increase of 3.8 per cent. This is not the only increase in the demand for food. It is felt that, with increased urbanisation and increased incomes, market demand for food would further go up.

---

1. FAO, *Third World Food Survey*, Basic Study No. II, Rome, 1963, p. 69.

During the last two decades, developing countries have made praiseworthy efforts to increase food production. But any gains have largely been offset by increase in population, and therefore the per capita food consumption has increased at a very moderate pace as compared to the more developed countries. The "Green Revolution" in India has provided the much-needed relief and has given a breathing space, but it does not provide a long-period solution of the problem.

Employment is another area of serious concern on account of rapid population growth. About two-thirds of the world's manpower resources are presently located in less developed countries. The working population in these areas will grow rapidly in the years to come, and is likely to double itself before the end of the century.

The sharp increase in the working population is chiefly due to the growing number of young people, but an increase in the length of working life, as a result of decline in mortality, is also a contributory factor. It has been estimated that, in less developed countries, the average number of working years for men will increase from 35.6 in 1960 to 38.9 in 1980 and 39.3 in the year 2000 A.D.

A demographic factor of considerable importance is the high dependency ratio in the less developed countries. The dependent population is about four-fifths of the size of the working population, while in industrialised countries it is only three-fifths. There is need, therefore, for developing labour-intensive and capital-saving methods of production and, in particular, smaller industries, labour-intensive and rural works, so that larger number of people can find employment.

Another major problem is of providing schooling to the growing number of school-going children in developing countries. During the period 1970-1980, the number of children of school age (5-14 years of age) increased from 640 million in 1970 to 822 million in 1980; and, according to the medium projects of the United Nations, will exceed 1,500 million by the end of the century, or nearly triple the present number.

The educational problems are not confined only to the young population. More than one-thirds of all the adults are also illiterate. In spite of vigorous literacy campaigns for adults and a decline in the percentage of illiterate adults from 43 per cent in 1950 to 39 per cent in 1960, the absolute number of illiterates is still increasing yearly by about 15 to 20 million, owing to rapid population growth.

Another important feature of the demographic situation in developing regions is the high rate of internal migration to urban areas, and a very rapid rate of growth of the cities and towns. It was estimated in early 1960's that nearly 10 dwelling units per 1,000 inhabitants had to be built each year in the developing countries[2] in order offset obsolescence and to cope with the urban population growth throughout the decade. In many countries only one-fifths of this goal has been accomplished. The housing situation has generally deteriorated and in some cases it is on the verge of disaster.[3]

There is a growing tendency for rural exodus to exceed employment opportunities generated in the urban areas by the development process. This tends to hamper economic growth because of increasing investments required for providing transport, housing, and other social services. Projections made by the United Nations indicate that during the 1960-70 and 1970-80 decades, the annual rate of growth of urban population in less developed regions would vary between 4.6 per cent and 4.5 per cent, whereas it will be between 2.1 per cent and 1.9 per cent in the more developed regions. While the population of localities with 20,000 inhabitants or more would triple in the coming three decades, the rural population will only increase by about 80 per

---

2. United Nation, *Housing, Building, and Planning in the Second Development Decade*, New York, 1972, p. 117.
3. United Nations, *Urban and Rural Population : Individual Countries*, New York, 1973, p. 12.

cent. Not only housing, but problems of drinking water, sewage disposal, sanitation, and transport, will also become more acute, and will require larger investments. Whatever little progress is made by these countries, it is almost eaten away by the growing population. Therefore it is a must to reduce population growth.

Demographic experts warn that the growth of the world population, which has surpassed the five billion, mark, is taking place mostly in Asian countries. The Second Conference of the Asian Forum of Parliamentarians on Population and Development held in Beijing declared 1988 as "The Day of the Three Billion". In 1987, the United Nations Fund for Population Activities (UNFPA) sponsored the "Day of Five Billion" which drew attention to these sobering statistics :

(a) World population is growing at the rate of 150 each minute, 2,20,000 each day and 80 million each year.

(b) World population has surged from two billion in the 1920s to three billion in 1960 and four billion by 1974. The last billion was added in 13 years, the next will come in 12 years.

(c) Ninety per cent of the growth has taken place in Asia, Africa and Latin America.

Figures crunched out by FAO's computer give the following major findings :

Land is limited. Only portion of the 2.99 billion hectares in the Asia, Africa and Latin America region (or 23 per cent of the world's total) can be put to crops. If areas under permanent pasture are added, some 46.5 per cent of the region's total land areas are presently utilised. But the rate at which land is being placed under permanent crops has decelerated.

These growth rates suggest that most of the small expansion in arable and permanently cropped land took place at the expense of areas previously under permanent pasture. Population is a major factor in this build-up of pressure on a static land-resource base.

Rapid population growth and falling incomes in terms of purchasing power are now reinforcing each other in developing countries. The largest landless and impoverished populations are concentrated in south Asia, principally on the Indian subcontinent. Thirty million landless represent close to 50 per cent of all rural households in South Asia. But rural landlessness is exacerbated by skewed land ownership in densely populated areas. It is usually only a matter of time until it translates into a decline in per capita income and into the need for food imports. The majority of regions have little additional land suitable for prudent agricultural use. As land runs out, countries have no option but to increase production on a shrinking resource-base. It is true that change in land arrangement and technology can achieve high rates of growth in agricultural production through intensive cultivation. The "Green Revolution" showed the way. Above all, it calls for the control of population to keep pace with the resources.

India as a whole, and Madhya Pradesh among States, have geared themselves up to confront these stupendous problems. A Central Family Planning Council presided over by the Union Health Minister, and consisting of all State Health Ministers and representatives of various organisations connected with family planning, reviews the implementation the programme, and lays down broad policies. State Family Planning Council exists in each State. In April 1966, a separate Department of Family Planning was constituted in the Ministry of Health at the centre to give technical and administrative direction and guidance to the programme and effect coordination of its various facts.

At the State level, the organisation set-up provides for a State Family Planning Bureau as part of the Directorate of Health Services, a District Family Planning Bureau for each district, Urban Family Welfare Planning Centres and City Bureaux for the urban population and Rural Family Welfare Planning Centres as integral part of the Primary Health Centres, with doctors and other staff to look after family planning and maternity and child health services. Under each Primary Health Centre, sub-centres are provided for every population of 10,000. Mobile services are also provided to fill the gap in services in the rural areas where static centres have not fully come into operation.

Communication for family planning is now being gradually integrated with the communication activities under different developmental programmes. This is being done to present family planning as a component of the total development programme, and not a programme in isolation. A high-powered interministerial multi-disciplinary and multi-professional Family Planning Communications Board was set up under the chairmanship of the Minister of Health and Family Planning in 1974 to implement the integration of the communications strategy. Consequently, the Department of Family Planning has commissioned the services of the Advertising Agencies Association of India, comprised of all the leading advertising agencies in India, to work out three experimental models of this communications strategy for the three States of Uttar Pradesh, Andhra Pradesh and West Bengal, and general kit of media mix for the rest of the country, to begin with.

All-India Hospitals Postpartum Programme was introduced in the National Family Planning Programme. The programme was started in 1969-70 in a modest way by covering only 59 institutions. With its successful implementation in these institutions, the programme was extended during 1971-73 period to cover another 65 institutions. The programme was extended to district level hospitals also. A Family Welfare Planning Centre has also been attached to each of the postpartum centres to provide follow-up and motivational services to the acceptors and also the population in the neighbourhood.

The Medical Termination of Pregnancy Act, 1971, came into force all over the country with effect from April 1982 except in the State of Jammu and Kashmir. Though mainly a health measure, it can also supplement family welfare planning.

Considering the importance of improving the health of mothers and children, and in view of its vital importance in the acceptance of the small-family norm, the maternity and child health programme has been integrated with the National Family Planning Programme. Besides providing normal MCH service, special emphasis is laid in the programme on :

(a) immunisation of children against diphtheria, whooping cough, and tetanus;

(b) prophylaxis against nutritional anaemia among mothers and children, and

(c) prophylaxis against Vitamin A deficiency diseases among children;

Nirodh is presently distributed all over the country through three schemes,, viz., (i) commercial distributed (ii) free supply scheme, and (iii) depot holder scheme. The oral pill programme gained momentum during the pilot project stage and was, consequently, extended in November 1974 to all urban family planning centres including local bodies, voluntary organisations, and to those primary health centres where the programme can be monitored and patients followed up. Steps have been taken to disseminate information to the general public on the availability of oral contraceptive pills under the National Family Planning Programme.

The role of the voluntary organisations in the promotion of family planning is well recognised. These organisations supplement official efforts in various ways, such as running urban Family Welfare Planning Centres and Auxiliary Nurse-Midwife Training Schools, conducting orientation-training camps and education services. Grants are released to various voluntary organisations and local bodies for family planning work.

Both employees and the organised working class in India have generally extended their support to the family planning programme. Organised sectors under the Government like the Railways and the Defence have an elaborate network of services for their own employees. The Post and Telegraph Department, theCoal Mines Welfare Organisation, the tea plantations in Eastern India and Southern India have drawn up extensive programme for family planning.

The Central Government has taken steps to associate recognised trade union leaders and workers' representatives in the implementation of the family planning programme. A committee of trade union leaders and Government of India was constituted some time back which has now been replaced by a Tripartite National Committee on Family Planning consisting of the representatives of the Government, Labour and Management, in addition to certain individual distinguished labour leaders. The committee would aid and advise the Government in the formulation and implementation of policies concerning the programme.

To help the programme reach the rural areas where bulk of the population lives, the Department has taken steps to involve Panchayati Raj institutions in the actual implementation of the programme. The Department of Community Development has been involved in this sphere.

The cooperative sector is being fully harnessed to popularise the concept of the small-family norm. Ways and means are being devised for active involvement of this sector.

Economic status

It is a notion universally accepted that poverty is the major cause of population increase. The most important factors leading to poverty are, first, poor land-man ratio; and, secondly, the illiteracy of the masses. Where land is scarce and limited, and illiteracy among men and women rampant, there is bound to be an increase in population. In industrially advanced societies, increase in population is not a problem, because of surplus resources.

On the other hand, there is a surplus of human resources in developing societies. Hence additional population is both the cause and effect of poverty. This increase in population is a hindrance to growth. It retards development in the following ways : (i) by pushing up demand, (ii) by reducing export potential, (iii) by leading to increase in imports, (iv) by making supply management difficult, (v) by causing inflation to become widely prevalent, (vi) by making unemployment widespread, (vii) by increase in unproductive labour, and (viii) by calling for more social expenditure on education, health, medicine, recreation, and the like

This is not to say that everyone in the society is poor. Yet it is true that, so long as people remain economically unsound due to unemployment or underemployment, or earn a deplorable low income, birth control publicity is likely to fall on deaf ears. Slum areas are comparatively less prosperous than non-slum areas. The slow pace of industrialisation in and around Hoshangabad has not improved the economic status of its inhabitants so much as that of the salaried and business class in relatively better industrialised proximate cities like Bhopal, Dewas, and Indore.

Table 23 summarises the data on the economic status of the slum respondents in urban Hoshangabad.

Table 23
HOSHANGABAD SLUMS : ECONOMIC STATUS

Family monthly income	*Respondents*	*Percentage*	*Ranking*
Unemployed	32	10.7	5
Below Rs. 1,000	73	24.3	1
Between Rs. 1,001 and Rs. 1,500	66	22.0	2
Between Rs. 1,501 and Rs. 2,000	54	18.0	3
Between Rs. 2,001 and Rs. 2,500	45	15.0	4
Above Rs. 2,500	30	10.0	6
Total	300	100	—

Source : Personal Investigation.

Vide Table 19, 29 or 9.7 per cent respondents were employees, 181 or 60.3 per cent were engaged in business, 58 or 19.3 per cent were involved in agriculture, while 32 or 10.7 per cent were out of employment. The present table does not offer any bright picture of the economic status of slum residents, because the largest proportion of 24.3 per cent among them have an income below Rs. 1,000 per month per family which, in these days of spiralling inflation, suggests that such families are living from hand to mouth and some of them are likely to be indebted.

The next highest proportion of 22 per cent slum families have an income varying between Rs. 1,001 and Rs. 1,500 per month which, again presents a bleak situation if the family happens to be a large one. Those with a family income varying between Rs. 1,501 and Rs. 2,000 per month constitute only 18 per cent in the sample survey which, according to slum standards, indicates a marginally better-off living standard. Another 15 per cent slum families earn between Rs. 2,001 and Rs. 2,500 per month, which suggests that the earning members of these families are in subordinate Government service, or in petty business, or small agriculturists cultivating their ancestral land. The few (10 per cent), whose family income is more than Rs. 2,500 per month, are relatively more prosperous in terms of slum life-style : they have more than one earning member and their total income, pooled together, exceeds Rs. 2,500 per month.

Small savings

For most people, savings represent the money that has been accumulated out of earned income, kept in a safe and secure place and can be reached quite easily if need arises. Investment is different in that it sets out not only to preserve capital but also to make it grow at the best pace possible coupled with the best security available. As a next step from savings, investment generally fetches a higher reward but entails a higher risk and demands a certain amount of specialised knowledge.

Whatever form our spare money takes, whether savings or

investments, it plays two vital and useful roles. For the individual, money set aside regularly from his earned income constitutes a reserve fund which can be drawn upon in times of emergency of which, if properly invested, yields a return. This return itself can be reinvested to add to the original capital or it may be used to meet some of the day-to-day expenses—an operation which has become increasingly necessary in these days of rapidly rising prices.

On the national plane, savings provide money to put up more defence establishments, build dams and irrigation canals, erect power houses and networks for the distribution of electricity, construct roads, build houses, hospitals and schools, establish water supply and drainage systems, prospect for oil and other minerals, build new factories or equip the existing ones with more machinery, and produce the many necessities of life. In other words, they help rapid industrialisation of the country and raise the standard of living of the common man.

While many people appreciate the importance of savings, and would like to save money, it is unfortunately true that only a small proportion of them is able to save at all. One reason for this is, of course, that many of us earn just enough to meet the daily expenses. But the reason why the rest, while having incomes above such marginal levels, cannot save is simply that they have no regular plan to save a certain amount at stated intervals.

To the query whether they saved any money, the answers of the slum respondents are indicated in Table 24.

Table 24

Question : Do you save any money ?

Do you save money ?	*Responses*	*Percentage*	*Ranking*
Yes	277	92.3	1
No	23	7.7	2
Total	300	100	—

Source : Personal Investigation.

The 10.7 per cent slum-residents are unemployed : it is therefore inconceivable that they should save. The monthly income of 24.3 per cent respondents is below Rs. 1,000, and hence saving is beyond their meagre means. Another 22 per cent slum resents earn between Rs. 1,001 and Rs. 1,500 per month which, keeping the ever-increasing inflation in mind, also leaves them out of the saving group. Yet another 18 per cent slum families earn between Rs. 1,501 and Rs. 2,000 per month. These numerically four-figure incomes are again offset by the interminable inflation. Thus, 75 per cent of the total slum residents in the sample survey are eliminated from the savers.

This leaves 15 per cent respondents whose family income ranges between Rs. 2,000 and Rs. 2,500 per month, and also 10 per cent families who earn more than Rs. 2,500 per month. Theoretically, they (15 per cent + 10 per cent = 25 per cent) are expected to save, but the table shows that, among them, the marginal proportion of 7.7 per cent families are savers, while the economic status of the overwhelming majority of 92.3 per cent slum families is so low that they are in no position to save at all. The purposes for which they save are dealt with in Table 25.

Reasons for saving

The hoarding of cash is neither desirable nor practical today. Money hidden in the proverbial mattress, under the carpet, in other supposedly safe and secret place, or carried about may be stolen, lost, or destroyed. Besides, users of capital are willing to pay a return for the use of our savings until we need them. Money hidden away brings no such return to the owner nor does it serve any useful purpose.

The accretion of savings with various institutions ultimately helps the individual to raise his living standard and the society to build itself on sound foundations. The banks finance various projects and self-employed entrepreneurs. The National Savings Organisation helps in building our defence, reconstruction, and development activities. Life insurance, besides giving the much-needed security to the individuals, helps the common man through its socially purposive investments. The Unit Trust helps in accelerating the pace of industrialisation, and thus brings in more employment opportunities and increased productivity.

The desire for security is an important force in the lives of the people. The quest for security involves many things, but one of the most important aspect is the search for financial security. One of the best approaches to financial security is through regular savings. The easiest way to ensure such savings is to make savings the first item of expenditure in our personal budget. Under the present conditions, it may be difficult to save after meeting day-to-day needs.

Table 25 shows where the small savers in Hoshangabad slums invest their savings.

Table 25

HOSHANGABAD SLUMS : INVESTMENT OF SAVINGS

Agency	*Respondents*	*Percentage*	*Ranking*
Unable to save	277	92.3	—
Investment in business	4	1.3	2
Provident Fund and other employees' welfare schemes	19	6.4	1
Bank	—	—	—
Post Office	—	—	—
Unit Trust	—	—	—
Any other	—	—	—
Total	300	100	—

Source : Personal Investigation.

Whatever allurement publicity for small savings may hold, the naked fact is that there must be some surplus left, after meeting day-to-day expenses, which one may save and, under proper guidance and supervision, invest and re-invest. To expect an average slum-dweller to save is to forget that he is a slum-dweller. Had his income been better, he would not be living in a slum.

The sample survey reveals that, while it is utterly beyond the capacity of the predominant majority of 277 or 92.3 per cent slum-residents to save, only 23 or 7.7 slum-residents do save. Among them the slender majority of 6.4 per cent, being employees of Government, semi-Government, or allied organisations, are under compulsion to save some money per month on account of statutory deductions from their salary in the form of contributions to provident fund and other schemes for the benefit of such employees. The microscopic minority of 1.3 per cent slum-dwellers invested whatever they happened to save in the petty business they were engaged in.

Summing up

It is the need of the hour that the family planning programme should become a people's revolution. Evidently, people would need to be motivated to a level where they would themselves seek out family planning services. The amount of work done during past years leads one to believe that the family planning programme in Madhya Pradesh is well on the way to becoming a people's revolution, for which it is essential to extend family planning services to the rural areas. The policy at present is to lay equal emphasis on both terminal and non-terminal methods of family planning, but it may become necessary to shift the emphasis to non-terminal methods in future for achievement of the objectives of the programme.

Expressed in simple terms, a doubling of population has occurred since independence. Many reasons are attributed to this slow decline in the birth rate. Improvement in nutritional levels, rising standards of living, and urbanisation trènds are believed to influence fertility decline positively. But age at marriage and literacy—specially female literacy—are considered to be the two most important contributors to fertility decline.

Postponement of marriage by women can have dramatic greater effect on population growth. The Child marriage Restraint Act was recently amended to prescribe the minimum age at marriage for males at 21 and for females at 18. Apart from the rigorous implementation of the Act, an educational process should highlight the ill effects of early marriage. The need to educate our people regarding the disastrous effects of early marriages among the illiterate requires coordinated efforts by the Public Health, Education and Tribal Welfare Departments. A strong link with the Social Welfare Department is also necessary because programmes for adult literacy and improving nutritional intake of women and children can be utilised to persuade women to adopt the small-family norm. Coordination among all these Departments is essential to convert the family planning movement into the people's revolution.

No revolution can succeed without the involvement of individuals and organisations outside the Government apparatus. Individual, social workers and social service organisations could render yeoman service by motivating acceptors and organising family planning camps. To coordinate and monitor family planning activities, District Collectors have been designated as the modal administrative authority in the districts for implementing the family planning programme. The Commissioners have been charged with responsibilities at the divisional level. The programme is being regularly monitored at the State level by the Health Secretary. At the highest level, the Family Welfare Council functions in the State under the Chief Minister. The Council is basically intended to elicit the largest measure of cooperation from the concerned departments of the Government, political parties, labour and industrial organisations, and social service organisations. Since the Divisional Commissioners are members of this Council, they have an opportunity to keep the Council informed of their field experiences, suggestions and difficulties. Ultimately, it is the people who must themselves feel convinced that small families are for their betterment. There are signs that this conviction is growing more among them.

Chapter VI

FAMILY PLANNING CONSCIOUSNESS AMONG SLUM FAMILIES

Has family planning failed ?

Family planning is not a failure in India. But there is an urgent need for fresh thinking on the family planning programme strategy. The programme should be viewed as a social and cultural revolution, aimed at changing the traditional values,and not as a medical programme. There is need for creating social consciousness so that young people consider it a patriotic duty to marry late and to have fewer children. The main reason for the rapid increase in India's population is a decline in the death rate, and not an increase in the birth rate. There are only two ways of reducing the birth rate : an increase in marriage age and use of contraceptives.Efforts in India should be concentrated on changing the atiitudes of the people.

"To plan when population growth is unchecked", according to the late Prime Minister Indira Gandhi, "is like building a house when the ground is constantly flooded".[1] According to her, family planning is an essential part of our strategy of enlarging welfare, Greater welfare is, in fact, the only reason for family planning; and we need it,not because "we are against more children, but because we want every child to have the best opportunity possible in life".[2]

India was the first country in the world officially to accept family planning as a welfare programme. Although family planning has been operative since 1951, it has been effective only since 1964-65. The extra-cautious and half-hearted approach of a realistic, coherent, firm and dynamic population policy, and a general unawareness on the part of the people were some of the reasons for the tardy progress of this national programme till about 1964. The nation paid heavily for the hesitancy and inaction during this period.

The fact of the matter is that demographic danger lies in the huge net additions made to the existing population of India from year to year and from decade to decade. The mounting population is illustrated below :

(a) 1891-1921 : An increase of 1.55 crores.

(b) 1921-1951 : An increase of 10.97 crores,

(c) 1951-1961 : An increase of 7.8 crores,

(d) 1961-1981 : An increase of slightly less than 11 crores.[3]

Can the Indian economy sustain this large population ? would not "Garibi Hatao" programme be in jeopardy ? What possibilities are there to have any rise in the per capita income ?

---

1. *Illustrated Weekly*, Bombay, 23 July 1988, p. 13.
2. Ibid., p. 12.
3. Ibid., p. 15.

Population limitation thus becomes inevitable, not only for survival, but also for the quality of survival, and there is no workable alternative to family planning. It is the gap between fertility rates and mortality rates that determines population growth. The concept of a large family, which was a common feature in India, irrespective of religion is no longer tenable. The age-old traditional religion-based advice to Muslims was : "When a servant of Allah marries, he perfects half his religion". But the advice was also followed by : "Produce if you can protect"[4] Social transformation is a slow process, but the large content of socially backward and economically weaker sections makes the task more difficult and the pace of social progress is rendered slower.

The Problem of population explosion, its consequences, and ways and means of arresting it have been subjected to much discussion in recent years in many a national and international forum. Both the developed countries and developing countries share this common concern, even though their demographic, socio-economic patterns, and the goals sought may be in sharp contrast. Any discussion on any aspect of family planning cannot avoid taking stock of the current demographic situation.

In the developing countries today, the rate of population growth varies mostly between 2 per cent and 3.5 per cent per annum.[5] With the control of disease through low-cost measures of public health and sanitation and fairly cheap and ready availability of medicines and effective antibiotics, mortality has been dramatically curtailed within a short period of time, resulting in this situation of greater survival and excessive growth of population. Falling mortality, combined with high fertility, has generated a structure with its consequent high dependency ratio.

Looking at the social and economic conditions, measured in terms of the per capita income, the level of literacy and labour force engaged in agriculture, as against industry, one is struck by the wide disparity in the socio-economic structure of

4. Ibid., p. 16.
5. *Journal of The Indian Medical Association*, vol. 59, No. 8, Calcutta, October 16, 1982, pp. 320-323.

the developing and developed countries. While the developing countries are confronted with the problem of numbers with a view to lift up their level of living subsistence, the developed countries approach the problem from above, so to say, in order to maintain, if not improve, the level of living they are already accustomed to. Besides, with industrialisation, there is the ever-increasing fear of depletion of natural resources, pollution or contamination or even extinction of nature's bounties like air and water, with their resultant adverse effect on the physical and psychological well-being of the people.

Attitude towards family planning

After covering the data relating to their personal, familial, and economic aspects of slum families, we come gradually and imperceptibly to the theme of family planning. The first question in this connection we asked the slum women was whether they favoured family planning or not. The responses to our queries are covered by Table 26.

Table 26

HOSHANGABAD SLUMS : RESPONSES TO FAMILY PLANNING

Response	*Respondents*	*Percentage*	*Ranking*
Yes	241	80.3	1
No	59	19.7	2
Total	300	100	—

Source : Personal Investigation.

The table elicits only the opinion regarding family planning among the slum inhabitants covered in our survey. It is silent upon the main question whether they practise family planning or not. One is entitled to have whatever opinion one has, but the crux of the matter lies in the fact whether one practises what one professes. The overwhelming majority of 80.3 slum women favoured birth control, which bears testimony to the extent of family planning awareness aroused among the residents of these sensitive areas, which are commonly believed to resist or sidetrack both planned parenthood education and measures.

Such large-scale awareness speaks of the vast amount of work done by family planning campaigners in these crucial areas which, not long ago, were notorious for indiscriminate breeding.

Part of this resistance is, however, still there, as evidenced by 19.7 per cent (almost one-fifths) of the slum women who told the investigator in unequivocal terms that they were against family planning, because of several plausible reasons—(i) that they were totally ignorant of the basics of family planning, (ii) that as family planning had never been practised in their family, the elders were opposed to it, (iii) that they found themselves to be too timid to talk to their elders about its necessity and the resultant advantages and disadvantages, (iv) that unless their husbands were won over to the concept of family planning, they were helpless and unable to involve themselves in it on their own, and (v) that they themselves were apprehensive of family planning, as it was something strange and novel for them which might have an adverse effect on their health and family life. It needs no reiteration that the majority of those who did not favour family planning were absolutely illiterate.

Age at marriage

The next important question, according to our interview schedule, was concerned with the age at which the slum women in our sample survey were married. The purpose behind this question was to ascertain whether the custom of early marriage still prevailed among the largely illiterate or semi-educated slum residents. Further, the age at which the girl marries has direct relevance with fertility rate. The earlier the age at which one marries, the more the likelihood of having more children. It is for this reason that family planning campaigners are canvassing through the media for marrying the girl when she is at least 18 and the boy when he is at least 21. Legislation to this effect has also been passed, but its implementation is not what it should be.

Theoretically, if a girl skips off marriage below the age of

18, she avoids adding one child to the growing population of the country. If she marries between 21 and 25, a couple of children are not added to the population growth. In other words, deferring marriage reduces the number of children, but this is not a very strong measure to reduce births, as the reproductive faculties of a woman normally continue until menopause which occurs when she has crossed her mid-forties.

Table 27 delineates data on the age at which the slum women of urban Hoshangabad were married.

Table 27

HOSHANGABAD SLUMS : AGE AT MARRIAGE

Age at marriage	*Respondents*	*Percentage*	*Ranking*
Below 18 years	122	40.7	1
Between 18 and 20 years	120	40.0	2
Between 21 and 25 years	58	19.3	3
Total	300	100	—

Source : Personal Investigation.

The table reveals that he age-old pernicious custom of marrying girls before they attain the age of 18 is still widely in vogue among the largely illiterate and semi-educated families living in the slums of urban Hoshangabad, as evidenced by a fairly large majority of 40.7 per cent girls who were united in wedlock in their tender teens. The stereotyped reasons for such marriages are hardly valid today. The hackneyed arguments commonly put forward are : (i) that girls are *paraya dhan* (the property of her would-be husband's family), (ii) that they are likely to go astray if they are not married early, (iii) that, on attaining the age of puberty, they are biologically fit to marry, and (iv) that it is the sons, and not the daughters, who perpetuate the family name.

Some of the slums in urban Hoshangabad have a mixed population of Hindus and Muslims. To make the legislation outlawing the marriage of minors, a correspondent from Madras cities the example of Pondicherry in his letter to the editor :

"In Pondicherry State, the registration of marriages of all communities and castes is compulsory. Before marriage, the proposed marriages have to be registered with the Registrar of Marriage Office. As far as Muslims are concerned, the Qazi performing the Ceremony is appointed and paid by the Government. On going to the registration department, the birth certificates of the bride and the bridegroom have to be produced to verify whether they have attained the age of 18 and 21, respectively. If they are below the prescribed age, registration is refused. The Qazi will not perform the marriage. This was the law before the merger and is still continuing. If such registration is made a law in other States and Union Territories, family planning may be better regulated."[6]

Another proportion of 40 per cent slum girls were married at an age varying between 18 years and 20 years, and thus were outside the purview of the legislation in respect of the marriage of minors. The minority of 19.3 per cent girls married at an age ranging between 21 years and 25 years, not largely because the slum families favoured late marriages, but mainly because many of them were unable to arrange the marriage of their daughter/daughters earlier.

Wife-husband age-difference

Brides younger than grooms by a few years are generally preferred in marriage, although there are rare exceptions where husbands are younger than their wives. In Indian society, the matrimonial preference for girls being rather younger than boys seems to be based on the fact that the tropical climate of the country generally makes women age faster than men in the sense that the bloom of their youth fades away quicker than that of men.

---

6. Abu Bakr, a. Muhammad, "Nikah Registration," *Radiance*, Delhi, 28 October-3 November, 1990, p. 11.

This may not, however, be wholly true in all cases. Malnutrition, insanitary living conditions, and frequent pregnancies my be the major contributory factors, individually, cumulatively, or both. Nutrition, a wholesome and hygienic environment, proper and regular fitness exercises, and good health go a long way in maintaining the figure and youthfulness of both women and men for a longer period. In terms of family planning, the age-difference between .wife and husband is relevant in the sense that the younger the wife, the greater the likelihood of more child births if planned parenthood is not accepted.

Table 28 presents data on the age-difference between wife and husband residing in the slums of urban Hoshangabad.

Table 28

HOSHANGABAD SLUMS : WIFE-HUSBAND AGE DIFFERENCE

Wife younger by	*Respondents*	*Percentage*	*Ranking*
Less than 3 years	62	20.7	2
Between 3 and 6 years	204	68.0	1
Between 6 and 9 years	29	9.7	3
Over 9 years	3	1.0	4
Both of equal age	2	0.6	5
Total	300	100	—

Source : Personal Investigation.

The table shows that the majority of 68 per cent slum women in urban Hoshangabad were younger than their spouses by the age-group ranging between 3 and 6 years. The next highest proportion of 20.7 per cent slum women were younger than their husbands by less than 3 years. In a few cases (9.3 per cent), the slum wives were younger than their husbands by the age-group varying between 6 and 9 years. The age gap between the spouses rarely extended over 9 years (one per cent) : it was zero when the almost negligible proportion of 0.6 per cent of married partners were of equal age.

The broad conclusion is that the general preference in

Hoshangabad city slums is that the bride should be younger than the groom by 3, 4, 5, or at the most 6 years. The table, however, does not indicate the age of the bride and the age of the groom at which both married, which could have enabled us in ascertaining the extent of the tradition of child marriages prevalent among the slum families of urban Hoshangabad.

Surviving children

The average no. of surviving children per family—plus the number of miscarriages, still births, or termination of pregnancy on medical grounds—present a fairly reliable scenario of the impact of the family welfare movement in the slums selected for study in urban Hoshangabad. Families favourably disposed to family planning justifiably tend to take into consideration the number of their surviving children, and then proceed to decide whether they want more children or whether the number of surviving children they have is enough and a full stop must be put to the birth of more children.

Table 29 provides sex-wise and age-wise data on the number of surviving children of the slum families of urban Hoshangabad.

Table 29
Hoshangabad Slums : Number of Surviving Children Sex-wise and Age-wise

Age-group	*Boys*	*Girls*	*Ranking*
1—5 years	182	178	2
6—10 years	210	213	1
11—15 years	141	140	3
16—18 years	37	41	4
Above 18 years	7	4	5
Total	577	576	—

Source : Personal Investigation.

The highest number of 210 boys and 213 girls, according to the table, fall under the relatively less vulnerable age-group of 6-10 years. The next highest group of 182 boys and 178 girls comes under the most vulnerable 1-5 years age-group. The third highest number of 141 boys and 140 girls is covered by the pre-adolescent age-group of 11-15 years. The minority of 37 boys and 41 girls fall under the adolescent 16-18 years. Only 7 boys and 4 girls had crossed he age of 18, the girls having legally attained the age of maturity.

In other words, the table highlights that the 300 slum families of urban Hoshangabad have a total of 1,153 surviving children. The number of male surviving children (577) almost equals that of female surviving children (576). The average number of surviving children per family works out to 3.84. This includes those families who have only one child (and may want one or two more) and also those who have 2, 3, 4, 5, and even 6 children. This calls for more intensive efforts to reduce child births either by non-terminal or by terminal methods, but preferably by means of the latter, specially by persuasion coupled with the temptation of incentives.

Place of baby's birth

The place government hospital, private maternity and nursing home, one's own residence or that of father/mother-in-law's—is an indication of the measure of care one would like to ensure in delivery. Individual attention and care is available in private maternity and nursing homes, though the bill one has to foot is quite inflated which only the very well-off can afford. Although expensive, there is little chance of complications being left unattended because a delivery in a maternity and nursing home takes place once in a while. In the maternity wards of a government hospital, there are general as well as a few private wards. While the general ward is free, the few private wards are less costly than the commercially run private maternity and nursing homes. Doctors, nurses, and midwives in government hospitals are skilled, but several deliveries occur there simultaneously all the twenty-four days. Delivery at one's residence or at that of father/mother-in-law's at the hands of the traditional midwives is often fraught with risk, as neither a qualified doctor nor equipment is at hand in one's own home or that of father/mother-in-law's in case of a sudden emergent situation.

To investigate whether the slum family takes care of the expectant mother at the time of the birth of a baby, we contacted the respondents and asked them where they usually went to have the child delivered. Their answers are processed in Table 30.

Table 30

HOSHANGABAD SLUMS : PLACE OF CHILD'S DELIVERY

Place of child's delivery	*Respondents*	*Percentage*	*Ranking*
Government hospital	86	28.7	2
Private maternity/nursing home	—	—	—
At own home	156	52.0	1
At father/mother-in-law's	58	19.3	3
Total	300	100	—

Source : Personal Investigation.

The table tells us that the majority of 52 per cent slum families have the child delivered at home, because they are either poor or have no time to take the would-be mother to the government hospital on account of last-minute labour pains. When the nearest midwife cannot be called instantly, experienced old women in the house or in the proximate neighbourhood substitute for the midwife as a make-shift arrangement.

The next highest proportion of 28.7 per cent slum families take the expectant mother to the Government hospital at Hoshangabad. There is almost cent per cent satisfaction from the maternity services offered by this hospital, where prenatal and postnatal services are also available, including sterilisation facilities.

The minority of 19.3 per cent slum families have the child delivered at the father/mother-in-law's home, especially the first child. It is an open secret that the expenses are borne, not by the husband and his family, but by the wife's family.

Mother's age at the birth of her first child

The age of the mother when her first child was born is, in general, a broad indicator of the approximate age at which she married. For example, if the age of the mother was below 16 years at the birth of her first child, the apparent inference is that she was married when she was legally a minor. If her age was somewhere between 18 and 30, the couple may have adopted birth control measures.

But the fact is that some women, without adopting planned parenthood, happen to conceive late and their first child is born after several years of marriage. A few women have some gynaecological defect and, until this is removed, their first child is born late. Similarly, a few men have some defect or the other affecting their reproductive capability which, when rectified, accounts for the late birth of their first child. When either of the couple is infertile, there is no child at all.

Table 31 furnishes data on the approximate age at which the slum mothers begot their first child.

Table 31

Hoshangabad Slums : Age at first Child's Birth

Age at first child's birth	*Respondents*	*Percentage*	*Ranking*
Below 18 years	21	7.0	3
18—20 years	210	70.0	1
21—25 years	66	22.0	2
26—30 years	3	1.0	4
Total	300	100	—

Source : Personal Investigation.

The table reveals that the large majority of 70 per cent slum mothers were between 18 and 20 years of age when their first child was born. If they were 18 years of age at the time they begot their first offspring, many of them must have been married when they were legally minors. If they were 20 when they gave birth to their first child, many of them were still teenagers at the time of marriage. A small proportion of 7 per cent mothers, who were below the age of 18, is clear evidence of child marriages. The broad inference, therefore, is that the undesirable custom of the marriage of minors and teenagers is widely prevalent among the slum residents of urban Hoshangabad.

A proportion of 22 per cent mothers delivered their first baby when they were between 21 and 25 years. This suggests either marriage on legally attaining the age of majority or the use of contraceptive devices. The minority of one per cent slum mothers who had their first child between the age of 26 and 30, either married late or were strict acceptors of family planning. It may also be that either they were suffering from some gynaecological disorder or their husbands were victims of some infirmity in their reproductive behaviour.

Mother's age at the birth of her youngest child

There is some point in asking a mother when her youngest child was born. On receiving her answer and, taking into consideration her present age and the number of children she has, she can be advised to have another child by proper spacing or to stop further childbirth (if she has more than 2 children) by taking to dependable contraceptives or by undergoing surgery.

Table 32 offers data on the approximate age at which the youngest child of slum mothers in urban Hoshangabad was born.

Table 32

HOSHANGABAD SLUMS : AGE AT YOUNGEST CHILD'S BIRTH

Age at youngest child's birth	*Respondents*	*Percentage*	*Ranking*
18—20 years	53	17.7	3
21—25 years	125	41.7	1
26—30 years	88	29.2	2
31—35 years	29	9.7	4
Over 35 years	5	1.7	5
Total	300	100	—

Source : Personal Investigation.

The table reveals that a large proportion of 41.7 per cent slum mothers were between the age of 21 and 25 when their youngest child was born, followed by 29.2 per cent mothers whose youngest child was born between the age of 26 and 30 years. The proportion of mothers belonging to the youngest age-group of 18-20 years when their youngest child was born works out to 17.7 per cent.

The minority of 9.7 per cent mothers were between the age of 31 and 35 years when their youngest child was born, while the minimal minority of 1.7 per cent mothers had crossed the age of 35 when they begot their youngest offspring.

These statistics suggest that all these age-groups are potential groups where family planning and family welfare education needs to be stepped up. Those mothers who were above 35 need to be reminded that, at their age, if they continue to have another child, they would be burdened with additional liability and they may grow too old to see their last child settled in life. The norm of a small family, not exceeding one or two children, must be made clear to them because, under the slum conditions in which they are living, they can ill afford to give more children better education and better opportunities in life, unless they are content to turn their children into mere replicas of their own selves. Commonsense demands that their succeeding generation must be better in many respects than they themselves.

Wanting more children

In the slum areas of urban Hoshangabad, small family units, with rather loose kinship ties, are the real pattern of life. Owing to this factor, the ideal the large joint family finds no takers in the slums. In most slum families, the individual occupies a fluid status, and many slum families seem to be reconciled to whatever status the urban non-slum society chooses to fit them in.

The disposition to high fertility among the slum residents may be due to several general factors : (i) slum parents expect children to look after them in old age, and (ii) in a situation where life offers hardship, sexual pleasure and having children are one of the few sources of satisfaction. Since high fertility is dominated by traditional attitudes and perceptions of supposed advantages, it will be naive to imagine that some parents are having more children than they desire and are only waiting for the family planning programme to save them from more children.

Table 33 records data on the responses to the query whether slum families wanted more children.

Table 33

QUESTION : DO YOU WANT MORE CHILDREN ?

Want more children ?	*Respondents*	*Percentage*	*Ranking*
Yes	53	17.7	2
No	247	82.3	1
Total	300	100	—

Source : Personal Investigation.

The table reveals that a small minority of 17.7 per cent slum mothers wanted more children. Most of them were in their early twenties, and many of them had one child which was not enough for them, as they put it. Where their sole child was a son, they wanted a sister for him, and where there only child was a daughter, they desired a brother for her, so that the sex difference could be equalised. A few who had a still birth or a miscarriage wanted a live-born child as a replacement.

But the large majority of 8.23 per cent slum mothers did not want more children, as they felt that they had enough. Most of these mothers were in their late twenties or early thirties. They had come to this conclusion either because of their own personal experience of hardship or because they had been influenced by the countrywide publicity commending birth control devices, the benefits of having a small family, and the immunisation of babies and expectant mothers.

Yet there seems to be a snag in their responses : *wanting*

no more children is one thing, *having* no more children quite another. In spite of not wanting, they may have children, unless they adopt terminal measures because, without doing so, "there is many a slip 'twixt the cup and the lip," as the significant saying goes.

Chapter VII

ADOPTION OF FAMILY PLANNING METHODS

The symbol of the red triangle is well-known. Each of its three sides represents a major field in which family planners are working. The first side stands for contraceptive technology and research in reproductive biology. There are a number of methods for preventing birth, but their proper use needs propagation. There are surgical methods (tubectomy and vasectomy), there are mechanical methods (condom and Copper T), and there are chemical methods (the pill).

The second side of the triangle represents the delivery of family planning and contraceptive services to the people. Family planning today is integrated with the general package of health and nutritional services. The idea that family planning is an independent programme, involving some kind of a vast give-away, is no longer valid. Family services have currently become part of the health structure, of which the apex is the All-India

Institute of Medical Sciences, but the roots are the primary health centres and sub-centres in the vast outreach.

The third side of the triangle implies motivation. The question in a democratic society is : how are we going to ensure that people take advantage of family planning services and that they are actually motivated towards the small-family norm ? This is the crux of the problem. Some people suggest that their should be compulsory sterilisation after two or three births. This means that people have to be motivated to accept a small-family norm voluntarily. For achieving this, all available means—the ratio, the television, the press, hoardings, person-to-person visits—all are utilised.

Slum residents : for and against family planning

If people are convinced that a smaller family has a better chance of attaining a decent standard of living, they will accept family planning. Interestingly enough, wherever there has been the green revolution, the population growth rate has fallen. Population and poverty are very closely interrelated. Historically, it was poverty that caused overpopulation Today, it is overpopulation that is contributing to poverty. This vicious circle has to be broken, and it can only be broken at he poverty end. We cannot kill people because we want to have less population. The answer to the problem lies in an integrated approach towards social transformation and economic development that includes the concept of family planning.

The people should be made to realise that children have a good chance of surviving, and that they are going to get the necessary inputs to live a decent life. After all, the children of today are the citizens of tomorrow. If the children are born warped, if their minds have not developed because of lack of nutritional inputs, and if their bodies are frail because they and their mothers have not been adequately fed, the future can never be bright. Every child must have the opportunity of growing into a full and healthy citizen, and to develop into a fully integrated human being.

Keeping this end in view, it was considered necessary to ascertain in clear terms the attitude of the slum residents of urban Hoshangabad towards family planning. Their responses *for* and *against* family planning are recorded in Table 34

Table 34

Slum Residents : Attitude to Family Planning

Attitude	*Respondents*	*Percentage*	*Ranking*
Yes	193	64.3	1
No	107	35.7	2
Total	300	100	—

Source : Personal Investigation.

In would be too much to expect 100 per cent family planning in any section of society, least of all in slum areas, so long as family planning remains voluntary. Yet much motivation work seems to have been done in bringing the slum residents closer to acceptance of family planning where they do not have to pay for anything out of their own pockets. This has been done so as not to put on them extra economic burden as well as to serve as an incentive. For example Nirodh and contraceptive pills (Mala) are distributed free, Copper T is inserted free and certain pain-relieving tablets are also dispensed free, while sterilisation is not only performed free but some amount of money is also presented as cash—partly as an incentive, and partly as compensation for the working day/days lost.

In this context, the table reveals that the majority of 64.3 per cent slum residents of urban Hoshangabad adopted family planning, but whether they continue to do so regularly or erratically is not clear from the table. The proportion of non-acceptors comes to the sizeable percentage of 35.7 (more than one-thirds of slum families), and it is these families on whom the family welfare workers have to concentrate more attention by removing their stock objections or genuine apprehensions through friendly discussion and persuasion in a language the slum parents easily understand.

Birth control measures by slum families

Time was when the public knew nothing about modern contraceptives, nor were there devices available over the counter. The woman was little better than a baby-manufacturing human machine. The sex act was, more or less hedonistic, leading to an annual bumper crop of babies in every locality. Repeated pregnancies enfeebled and emaciated the woman, and maternal mortality rate raced with that of infant mortality. The deceased wife was lamented for a brief period, and was soon replaced by a young new wife who was destined to meet a no better fate. The last 40 years or so saw an unprecedented reawakening among men and women. The aggressive publicity of the family planning programme during the last two decades cautioned couples against the perils of repeated pregnancies and educated them on the methods of spacing children.

Among the devices to prevent births, the most effective is sterilisation : it solves the problem once and for all. It is therefore of the utmost significance that special incentives be offered to attract the people to this method. For its success and popularity, it is necessary that competent doctors and nurses and good equipment are provided. Small failures in this field will jeopardise the entire scheme. Hence no price is toohigh to avoid such risks of failure.

Table 35 registers the response of 193 slum families to birth control methods which they have adopted.

Table 35

HOSHANGABAD SLUMS : BIRTH CONTROL METHODS ADOPTED

Method adopted	*Respondents*	*Percentage*	*Ranking*
Against family planning	107	35.7	—
Natural methods			
(i) Celibacy (Brahmacharya)	—	—	—
(ii) Late marriage	—	—	—
(iii) Moral restraint	—	—	—

Method adopted	*Respondents*	*Percentage*	*Ranking*
Biological methods			
(i) Coitus interruptus	—	—	—
(ii) Rhythm method	—	—	—
Chemical methods			
(i) Foam tablets	—	—	—
(ii) Jelley	—	—	—
(iii) Oral pills	23	7.7	4
Mechanical methods			
(i) Diaphrams	—	—	—
(ii) Condom	—	—	—
(iii) Intrauterine device	29	9.6	3
Surgical methods			
(i) Vasectomy (male surgery)	54	18.0	2
(ii) Tubectomy (female surgery)	87	29.0	1
(iii) Medical termination of pregnancy	—	—	—
Total	300	100	—

Source : Personal Investigation.

The table brings out a clear picture before us. Slum residents in urban Hoshangabad (with 29 per cent women undergoing tubectomy and 18 per cent men submitting to vasectomy, thus accounting for a total of 47 per cent family planning acceptors) tend to prefer a permanent method of averting future births to the temporary ones, having been persuaded by family planning campaigners to come to this irreversible decision after they had achieved the small-family norm which, in their case, lay between one child and 3 children.

The lesser proportion of 17.3 per cent slum women (7.7 per cent using oral pills and 9.6 per cent accepting Copper T, also inserted free) have adopted these temporary devices, probably to space children under advice offered to them by others. The extent of male domination in slum families is evidenced by the fact that, out of 193 or 64.3 per cent family planning acceptors, the proportion of women was the largest (139 or 46.3 per cent), which suggests that more men tend to put their women under birth control restrictions, and that it is only a few men (54 or 18 per cent in the sample survey) who, sparing their women, take the entire burden of family planning upon themselves.

In this regard, it would not be out of place to mention the new fertility methods which are more being explored. In the 1960s, oral contraceptives and intrauterine devices were introduced to control reproduction. The international community by then had come to realise the dangers inherent in a rapid demographic growth. But this was just a breakthrough which would one day lead to fertility regulation.

Fertility regulation is a broader concept which includes control of fertility as also the promotion of fertility. The promotion of fertility applies to those who, for certain biological reasons, cannot have children. The advancement in the science of test-tube babies would enable any family that desires children to have them. A large number of laboratories are engaged in this research, but so far the success achieved is only 17 per cent to 20 per cent.

Fertility control as we all know, are ways of controlling reproduction. The methods in use are, however, not foolproof. Therefore alternative ways are being explored which would be more effective, with no side-effects. RU-486 is one such contraceptive being experienced on in the laboratories. It would be a pill for women, and probably would not be cancerous. This contraceptive has, however, been objected to by the French.

Other researches are being carried out in the field of intercepting the process of maturation of the sperm in the man's body. An immature sperm would not be productive. While in the female body, where the embryo development takes place, researchers are working on the signals that the body gives for its development. If these signals could be identified, unwanted pregnancy could be avoided.[1]

Regular/irregular use of contraceptives

No one can deny that sex is one of the prime forces behind innumerable actions and reactions. Life is related, in an intricate manner, to the functioning of sex. Scientific and clinical studies of sex apart, there seems to prevail a self-willed attitude among laymen which stresses sensual enjoyment as the most important experience of life.

Every human being, man or woman, passes through various stages of sexual development from adolescence to old age. In youth, sexual maturity is followed by the sexual urge. Gradually, this longing for sex leads to heterosexual attachments and results in sexual fulfilment. Every society provides for the natural growth of sexual fulfilment within the framework of marriage partnership. When sex results in conception and reproduction, the care of the offspring becomes an important matter which cannot be overlooked. The child's dependence on its parents, for the most part of its childhood, makes it imperative for sex to be given legal and social sanctions within a stable man-woman partnership.

All couples have therefore the basic right (i) to decide freely and responsibly the number and spacing of their children, and (ii) to have the information, education, and the means to do so. The responsibility of couples, in the exercise of this right, takes into account the needs of their living and future children as well as their responsibilities towards the society.

Table 36 sums up the data on whether the family planning acceptors use contraceptives regularly or erratically.

---

1. "New Fertility Control Methods Being Explored," *The Statesman*, 10 November, 1990, p. 4.

Table 36
HOSHANGABAD SLUMS : USE OF CONTRACEPTIVES : REGULAR OR IRREGULAR

Conceptive use—regular	*Respondents*	*Percentage*	*Ranking*
Yes	40	13.3	1
No	12	4.0	2
Sterilised	141	47.0	—
Non-acceptors	107	35.7	—
Total	300	100	—

Source : Personal Investigation.

The table reveals that, out of 300 slum families, the proportion of non-acceptors equalled 35.7 per cent, while those of the sterilised totalled 47 per cent. This leaves us with 17.3 per cent women contraceptive-users (7.7 per cent of those taking oral pills plus 9.6 per cent of those with Copper T insertions). Among these, 13.3 per cent were using contraceptive regularly, while the marginal proportion of 4 per cent used their contraceptive irregularly. The irregular use temporary contraceptives may be attributed to their main purpose of spacing children. When they want to have a child, the women stop taking pills or get the Copper T taken out. Some slum women also answered that on some day they forgot to take their daily pill.

Reasons for not favouring family planning

The non-acceptors of family planning in Hoshangabad slums were asked why they did not favour family planning. They were hesitant to answer this simple question, because of the sensitivity and privacy of their sexual life coming out in the open. We, therefore, came to their rescue by suggesting to them 3 readymade answers which, we thought, were generally applicable to illiterate and semi-literate slum women. These readymade answers were (i) You have not enough information about family planning, (ii) You do not enjoy sexual life, or (iii) Two or three children are not enough. To choose one of these answers, therefore, became easier for them.

Table 37 presents data on the reasons underlying the anti-family planning attitude of the slum residents of urban Hoshangabad.

Table 37

HOSHANGABAD SLUMS : REASONS AGAINST FAMILY PLANNING

Reasons	*Respondents*	*Percentage*	*Ranking*
Not enough information about family planning	88	29.3	1
Do not enjoy sexual life	17	5.7	2
2 or 3 children are not enough	2	0.7	3
Family planning acceptors	193	64.3	—
Total	300	100	—

Source : Personal Investigation.

The table shows that, out of the 300 slum families included in our sample survey, only 107 or 35.7 per cent were against family planning. Of these, the proportion of 29.3 per cent women frankly admitted that they knew nothing about the ins and outs of family planning. The smaller proportion of 5.7 per cent women confessed that once or twice when their husband resorted to withdrawal as a means of averting conception, while others said that a few times when their husband use a condom, both of them did not enjoy sexual relation as they used to enjoy it before, and therefore both of them had returned to their former practice.

The almost neglible proportion of only 2 or 0.7 per cent slum wives were against family planning for different reasons. One was of the opinion that 2 or 3 children were not enough for her, because she was not sure that everyone of them would survive. The other said that her children had grown big, and she wanted another baby of her own to play with as she used to do when her children were infants : to her, children about the age of four or five were sweeter than children above that age because older children were a constant headache to her for being willful and disobedient.

Desire for a child of the opposite sex

About 2 or 3 decades ago, the general trend among many families was that, if they had a daughter, they hoped that their next child would be a son. When the second child also happened to be a daughter also, they again hoped that the next would be a son, and so on. The writer knows a family which, in the hope of having a son had 5 successive daughters whose marriage prospects, because of the dowry system, worried them a great deal. Finally, the father was persuaded to be content with his 5 daughters and undergo vasectomy, which he did.

On the other hand, the writer also knows 4 families which had 2 daughters each and, without being desirous of a son, they took to family planning. The writer further happens to know a family which believed in the one-child norm. The child happened to be a son, and when he grew up to be about 10, the parents felt that they needed a sister for him. They suspended family planning and, when their next child chanced to be a pretty girl, they threw a lavish party on the occasion, and have readopted planned parenthood.

These experiences of the writer prompted her to ask the slum families of urban Hoshangabad : "If you have 2 or 3 children of the same sex, will you try to have one more child of the opposite sex ?" The responses of the slum residents are registered in Table 38.

Table 38

Desiring a Child of the Opposite Sex

Responses	*Respondents*	*Percentage*	*Ranking*
Yes	39	13.0	2
No	68	22.7	1
Family planning acceptors	193	64.3	—
Total	300	100	—

Source : Personal Investigation.

The majority of 64.3 per cent family planning acceptors informed the investigators that they had children of both sexes. Only a few had sons, and another few only daughters. They said that the number of children they had was enough, and it was immaterial for them if they happened to have no child of the opposite sex.

The non-acceptors of family planning, were, however, divided over this issue. While 22.7 per cent of them seemed to echo the message of 1990 as the SAARC year of the girl child, the minority of 13 per cent insisted that, in their opinion, there must be at least a boy if their other children were all girls, and at least one girl if their other children were all boys, because brother-sister ties not only help the proper psychological growth of children but think relationship also proves useful in future years.

Impact of family planning on sex life

The adoption of family planning on the part of the newly initiated is fraught with several preconceived fears. Some apprehend that man-made change in their reproductive life is contrary to nature. Others are afraid that their manhood or womanhood, being encroached upon, will decrease the virility of men and negate the willing cooperation of women. Still others cherish the baseless fear that deliberate interference in their reproductive function will have an undesirable impact on their reproductive behaviour.

We, therefore, considered it pertinent to inquire of the slum couples whether adoption of family planning made their sex life better or worse than before, and whether it remained unchanged. Their responses are recorded in Table 39.

According to the table, the anti-family planning families in Hoshangabad slums totalled 35.7 per cent. This left us with the figure of 64.3 per cent, comprising of families which had adopted planned parenthood. A few weeks after taking up either terminal or non-terminal measures, the largest proportion of 43 per cent

Table 39

IMPACT OF FAMILY PLANNING ON SEX LIFE

Effect	*Respondents*	*Percentage*	*Ranking*
Better than before	64	21.3	2
Worse than before	00	00.0	—
Unchanged	129	43.0	1
Non-acceptors	107	35.7	—
Total	300	100	—

Source : Personal Investigation.

respondents said that their sexual life remained unchanged. This gives the lie to the general belief prevailing among some conservative men that vasectomy would effect their manhood adversely and also among orthodox women that tubectomy, being an offence against nature, nature will have its revenge.

Another sizeable proportion of 21.3 per cent women confessed that they felt better than before. Asked to elaborate further, they said that, being no longer afraid of an unwanted pregnancy, they enjoyed sex life better than they did when they were in constant fear of conceiving against their will.

Signs of change after adoption of family planning

Many misconceptions about family planning adoption prevail among the unknowing masses. Some of the ignorant among the family planning adopters, especially women, complain of pain, particularly in the abdomen and the back. In addition to this, others complain of nausea and headache. Some others complain of deterioration of health. But according to family planning experts most of these complaints as an aftermath of family planning are not genuine : many of them are purely imaginary based on vitiated psychology.

Table 40 reproduces data in respect of any change, or physical discomfort, or changes after the adoption of family planning by the slum families of urban Hoshangabad.

Table 40

CHANGE AFTER FAMILY PLANNING ADOPTION

Signs of change	*Respondents*	*Percentage*	*Ranking*
Any pain			
Increased	36	12.0	4
Reduced	00	00.0	—
Same	61	20.3	1
Condition of health			
Increased	38	12.7	3
Reduced	00	00.0	—
Same	58	19.3	2
Any other			
Increased	00	00.0	—
Reduced	00	00.0	—
Same	00	00.0	—
Non-adopters	107	35.7	—
Total	300	100	—

Source : Personal Investigation.

The table unravels a fluctuating pattern of responses. While 12 per cent of adopters of family planning complained of pain, the large proportion of 20.3 per cent confessed that there was no change in their condition : it was the same as before. The truth of the matter is that those women who had Copper T inserted admitted that they did feel somewhat uncomfortable during the first few days, but afterwards felt quite normal. There is also some pain after vasectomy when the effect of the local anaesthesia wears off, and there is also some pain in tubectomy when the woman wakes up from anaesthesia. As long as the incision is not fully healed, the pain is bound to persist. Once the wound fills itself up and the stitches are removed, there should be no reason to feel any pain, unless something has gone wrong in the surgical operation.

Similarly, while nobody complained that his or her health was reduced, 12.7 per cent slum respondents said that there was neither improvement nor deterioration their health.

The reason is not far to seek. Improvement in health may be due to the extinction of the fear psychosis arising from an wanted pregnancy.

Family planning methods : easier for men or women ?

At the moment, the family planning approach suffers from gender bias. Women's organisations are justified in protesting against the policies that play with the lives of women, especially in the matter of sterilisations. It is time to bring men to the operating table, not because women feel that men should be put equally at risk, but simply because vasectomy is much simpler, quicker, and less expensive procedure than tubectomy. It is important to generate awareness that too many births are detrimental not only to the mother but also to the entire family—sons and husband included. Family planning is not a woman's problem alone. Women constitute a group that normally does not have the last word in these matters, even if it is the most affected by the decision.

The estimates of the Eighth Plan reveal that there will be 33 million more people by the year 2000 than was projected in the Seventh Plan, bringing the total to 1.18 billion. Hopes of achieving zero population growth have thus been pushed back a decade, and may now be possible only by 2011-2016 A.D.[2] This, too, if targets met on paper square with the actual achievement on the ground. At present, the achievement of the couple protection rate of 35 per cent is not reflected in the slowing down of the birth rate. Besides, we are nowhere near the goal of 60 per cent couple protection rate by the turn of the century, now only 10 years away. The awareness that we multiply ourselves only to divide the gains must lead to a sound and feasible policy, and not remain an academic numbers game.

Keeping these points in mind, we discussed with our slum respondents, both men and women, which among the permanent and temporary methods of family planning was easier for men,

2. *Times of India*, New Delhi, 4 October, 1989, p. 10.

and which for women. The answers we received are presented in Table 41.

Table 41

FAMILY PLANNING METHODS : EASIER FOR MEN OR WOMEN ?

Family planning methods	*Respondents*	*Percentage*	*Ranking*
Permanent methods for men	54	18.0	2
Permanent methods for women	87	29.0	1
Temporary methods for men	00	00.0	—
Temporary methods for women	52	17.3	3
Non-adopters of family planning	107	35.7	—
Total	300	100	—

Source : Personal Investigation.

The table reveals that, as compared to 29 per cent slum women who had undergone tubectomy in urban Hoshangabad, only 18 per cent men had submitted to vasectomy. This suggests that slum men had not yet come to realise that sterilisation was easier for them, because (i) it takes less time, (ii) it is not a complicated procedure, (iii) it is less expensive for the government, (iv) it enables the man to return to work earlier, and (v) it does not affect vitality at all.

Some men thought that sterilisation of women was easier after the delivery of the last of the required number of children, because the mother is still at the hospital and her physiological condition is most appropriate for tubectomy. This argument is true, but it betrays selfishness of the male who still wants to retain his reproductive capacity for reasons deeply hidden in his heart.

As regards temporary methods of family planning, there was near unanimity that they were good only for the purpose of spacing children, and not for bringing about the final termination of births. None of the men in the slums indicated his preference for condom (Nirodh). Some slum women were also sceptical about the oral contraceptive pill (Mala). Very few women willingly favoured IUD (Copper T). The proportion of those who regarded temporary methods easier for women was the least in the sample—only 17.3 per cent. A few respondents reported that a double safety measure lay in the adoption of Nirodh by the husband as well as the regular intake of the pill by the wife.

Personal reaction to the adoption of family planning methods

The adoption of family planning methods induces certain diverse reactions among the adopters, both men and women. After all, it is something artificial, a deliberate obstruction against the normal operation of the reproductive laws ordained by nature. The adopter may feel embarrassed or sad, proud, or just normal. The feeling, whatever it be, is likely to be strong initially, but with the passage of time it begins to wane away and finally disappears altogether.

All married couples tend to experience such feelings, but the younger couples do so more strongly. Those who are sterilised experience these emotions most prominently than those who adopt temporary methods. The natural reaction is one of embarrassment. The more negative reaction is that of regret at the permanent loss of fertility. The positive reaction is one of pride generated by a sense of achievement. For some men and women, there is hardly any lingering reaction and they feel quite normal as they were before.

Table 42 brings out the reaction of the slum respondents of urban Hoshangabad to the adoption of family planning methods.

The table unfolds that a small proportion of 6 per cent family planning adopters in the slum areas of urban Hoshangabad felt quite normal. They complained of loss neither of virility nor of pleasure. They were not self-conscious of any truncation of their manhood or womanhood or of any split in their personality. it seems that they had been made to understand their own limitation with regard to the optimal size of the family within

Table 42

PERSONAL REACTION TO FAMILY PLANNING ADOPTION

Personal reaction	*Respondents*	*Percentage*	*Ranking*
Embarrassed	102	34.0	1
Sad	58	19.3	2
Proud	15	5.0	4
Normal	18	6.0	3
Non-adopters	107	35.7	—
Total	300	100	—

Source : Personal Investigation.

their means, the importance of their own health as fathers and mothers, and the general physical, mental, and educational welfare of their children.

The smallest proportion of only 5 per cent slum men and women, after they recovered from sterilisation, felt a sense of pride in overcoming obstactles and objections, in having successfully carried out what they regarded as a personal and family necessity, in feeling liberated from the future bondage of child birth and child-rearing with the attendant responsibilities and anxieties, and in having secured in their opinion a better future for themselves and their children.

The highest proportion of 34 per cent adopters of family planning felt quite embarrassed at what they were doing, at least in the initial stages. They were sometimes nervous in the beginning, always conscious that the Copper T or the Mala pill was there. Those who had offered themselves for sterilisation were also nervous and somewhat afraid at the outset, but after some time it was smooth sailing for them. The embarrassment arose not only from what others would say if they came to know but also from the fact that what they were doing was what they had never done before nor their parents (to the acceptor's best knowledge and belief) had practised before.

Another proportion of 19.3 per cent from among the 47 per cent sterilised men and women in the slums experienced a feeling of regret that they would have no more babiesand what would happen if those they had happened to die. The fear of the unknown future, the apprehension of the unexpected and possible death of their child/children, the realisation that in such an event there would be no one to continue the family name and to inherit whatever they have—all these latent fears had a combined force which led them to a feeling of regret or sadness.

Reaction of elders

Ascertaining the reactions of elders in the family to the planned parenthood devices adopted by their married children indicates the extent to which family planning and family welfare programme has caught up in the slum areas of urban Hoshangabad. It is no secret that many of these elders are out of tune with the times and still cling to their cherished concept of a world that has vanished with their passing years for ever. They believe that conception and delivery should run their natural course, and that any attempt to stop or alter the reproductive functions of a human being is an offence against nature and an unpardonable sin in the eyes of God Almighty which may deprive them of a comfortable berth in heaven. Although some of them do not say so in so many words, they decry family planning devices on one lame excuse or another.

This by no means implies that unobstructive elders do not exist. It is no secret that some elders even in slum areas, unless they are senile, are fairly receptive to the changing ideas of their progeny. In the course of their years, they have become adequately are of the prevailing economic and housing compulsions that tend to favour a small-size family. In conforming to the wishes of their married sons and daughters perhaps they wish to atone for the mistakes of their own days when there was no exposure to fertility control publicity.

Table 43 covers data on the reaction of family elders to the use of birth control measures.

Table 43

HOSHANGABAD SLUMS : REACTION OF ELDERS TO BIRTH MEASURES CONTROL

Reaction of elders	*Respondents*	*Percentage*	*Ranking*
Favourable	64	21.3	2
Unfavourable	129	43.0	1
Non-acceptors	107	35.7	—
Total	300	100	—

Source : Personal Investigation.

The table deals with 193 or 64.3 per cent adopters of family planning in the slum areas of urban Hoshangabad. The data do not show a very wholesome trend. Only 21.3 per cent elders reacted favourably to the fertility control measures adopted by their married children, while the majority of 43 per cent reacted against what they termed "unnatural devices". Among those whose reactions were favourable, the writer knows a few elders who had five or more children, admitting they are happy that their married children favour a restricted family.

Some obstructionist elders are not content to register their protest verbally. When, in the teeth of the opposition, a young married member of their family, particularly their married daughter, undergoes family planning surgery, they make no attempt to conceal their displeasure and distaste for the son-in-law who induced his wife to opt for sterilisation. As it is, conversation with the interviewers revealed that, in many cases, the parents of the girl secretly wished that the son-in-law should undergo surgery, while the parents of the boy wished in their heart of hearts that it is the daughter-in-law who should have undergone sterilisation.

Hesitation in admitting practising family planning

Asking one whether he or she practises family planning is an intensely personal question. The respondent hesitates before a stranger, but shows no hesitation when the questioner is a familiar person. Family planners will frankly confess that they practise family planning, even naming the devices, to those with whom they are on intimate terms. But nothing is hidden from those who attend to them when they are being sterilised and from those who take the woman to the hospital or the health centre for contraceptive pills or for Copper T insertion. These persons tell others, and gradually the entire slum area comes to know who is doing family planning and in which manner.

Table 44 covers responses to the query whether the respondents had any hesitation in saying clearly that they practised family planning.

Table 44

QUESTION : DO YOU HAVE ANY HESITATION IN SAYING CLEARLY THAT YOU PRACTISE FAMILY PLANNING ?

Any hesitation ?	*Respondents*	*Percentage*	*Ranking*
Yes	74	24.7	2
No	119	39.6	1
Non-acceptors	107	35.7	—
Total	300	100	—

Source : Personal Investigation.

The table reveals that the majority of 39.6 per cent practitioners of planned parenthood feel no hesitation when they are asked whether they practise family planning because, in their opinion, no purpose is served in hiding what happens to be a fact, and not a taboo, what is not only legal but is also widely promoted by family planning programmers.

It is only the minority of 24.7 respondents, largely the slum women, who hesitate to give a candid answer, especially to outsiders, to remote relatives, and to distant visitors with whom they are not on close terms.

Decision-makers of the size of the family

In big urban areas, the number of educated people is fairly large, some of them being very highly educated. For this reason, they do not need motivated from the outside : they are, by the large, self-motivated, and it is therefore either the husband or the wife, or other, who decide the size of the family. But in the slum areas of these very towns it is the other way round. It is usually the staff of the family welfare department who determine the size of a slum family in the sense that, when they see a poor family with many children or likely to have many children, they attempt to persuade it to go in for planned parenthood. Sometimes, it is the other members of the family who, being family planning practitioners themselves and realising the advantages accruing to them, try to win over a particular family in which they are interested to restrict the family size by adopting family planning measures.

Table 45 provides data on those who decided to limit the size of the family of slum respondents in urban Hoshangabad.

Table 45

DECISION-MAKERS OF THE FAMILY SIZE

Decision-makers	*Respondents*	*Percentage*	*Ranking*
You yourself	00	00.0	—
Government	185	61.6	1
Husband/wife	2	0.7	3
Other family members	6	2.0	2
Non-acceptors	107	35.7	—
Total	300	100	—

Source : Personal Investigation.

The table reveals a pattern which is not very encouraging. In the largest number of 61.6 per cent cases, it were the family planning canvassers who had persuaded the slum families to take recourse to planned parenthood to limit the size of their family. The small proportion of only 2 per cent slum families reported that they had come round to the practice of family planning on the persuasive advice tendered by some other members of the family. It is only a fractional minority of only 0.7 per cent respondents, all of them mothers of several children, who took the decision to halt the size of the family only after it was becoming quite unmanageable for them. The broad conclusion emerging from these responses is that the slum residents, although they may have been awakened to the consciousness of the merits of a small family, yet lack the initiative to come forward to adopt family planning measures themselves : they still need the goading of others.

Feeling free after using a family planning method

In theory, those who use a family planning method ought to feel free, but in actual fact this is not so. Those who make use of temporary measures are not sure of their 100 per cent reliability. If there occurs an interval when the pill was not taken, either by negligence or it being not at hand, the peril of an unwanted conception always lurks at the back of the woman's mind.

Further, vide Table 41, as many as 58 or 19.3 per cent men and women regretted having got sterilised themselves for fear that death may lay its icy hands on their child/children and, in that eventuality, having meddled with their reproductive functions, they would not be able to have a replacement. Needless to say that such fears are without foundation and a pure concoction of their morbid imagination. There is no reason why, with proper nutrition, hygienic care, and health management, any child should die.

Table 46 considers data on responses of the slum families of urban Hoshangabad with regard to the feeling of freedom they enjoy after using a family planning method.

The table eliminates 107 or 35.7 per cent families who are currently hostile to family planning. Some of them are, however, likely to cross the floor in future when hard pressed by necessity to do so. We find that a proportion of 19.3 per cent slum couples, many of whom sterilised, did not feel any sense of liberation from the thraldom of child births and child-rearing. Haunted by doubts regarding the survival of their

Table 46

QUESTION : DO YOU FEEL MORE FREE AFTER USING A FAMILY PLANNING METHOD ?

Feel more free ?	*Respondents*	*Percentage*	*Ranking*
Yes	135	45.0	1
No	58	19.3	2
Non-acceptors	107	35.7	—
Total	300	100	—

Source : Personal Investigation.

offspring/offsprings, they were most anxious when their child fell ill. An indirect benefit of this illness was that they gave the child the best medical treatment within their limited means and also the most careful nursing at home, heaving a sigh of relief when the child retrieved its health.

But the largest proportion of 45 per cent adopters of family planning methods, after having overcome their initial embarrassment or nervousness, enjoyed the feeling of freedom that goes with the regular use of a family planning method. This was evident from their faces, their conversation, and their behaviour which was no longer darkened by clouds of fear.

Summing Up

According to a Press Trust of India report, Indian scientists are testing a new anti-pregnancy pill (RU-486) which replaces surgery for abortion and offers hope to developing countries searching for a safe and effective method of family planning. RU-486 was first developed in France and attracted world-wide attention, as it offered a self-administered method of family planning and terminating pregnancies that eliminates the need to go to a doctor. The pill is available in France and China and is expected to hit the market in Sweden shortly.

Doctors at the Institute of Research in Reproduction, Bombay, are working on animals to study the possible use of RU-486 as an antipregnancy pill. The findings of the studies were presented at the International Conference of Frontiers in Reproductive Physiology which concluded at Bombay on 10 November 1990. RU-486 works by blocking the natural action of a hormone progesterone which helps in maintaining pregnancy. The pill induces abortion in 80 per cent of the cases when given during the early stages of pregnancy, and in 58 per cent of the cases when given in the later stages after 42 days.

The pill, which can be taken orally, is rapidly absorbed in the blood stream. Only 40 per cent is available for biological action, the rest being degraded the liver. Reported side-effects include minor pains, cramps, and nausea.[3]

Chapter VIII

INCENTIVES AND FAMILY PLANNING

Till now the advancement of science and technology has enabled man to augment substantially the availability of food. But the sum total of the available natural resources being constant, a time should come when further innovations are not possible even to maintain the break-even level, if the number of persons keeps on growing endlessly, unless of course one expects the Malthusian positive checks to take hold of the situation. When reduction in mortality has been accepted as a desirable goal under any circumstances, it is obvious that there is no other way to realise the goal of containing the population growth than to wage an all-out war on fertility.

Inter-relationships of demographic and socio-economic variables are complex, and current researches on them are still rudimentary, particularly with regard to the developing countries. But the studies made so far do indicate that a reduction in fertility, besides checking the numbers, has the advantage of hastening and sustaining a faster rate of economic development, whose impact is increasingly felt in the long run. It has also been shown that dampening of population growth is likely to produce a developed economic structure with increasing effective demand due to a sustained increase in per capita income. With more balanced income distribution, the industrial transportation, and communication sectors will have a greater impetus to grow thereby facilitating large-scale production.

It was this realisation of the need for containing the population through controlled fertility which prompted India to embark upon family planning as an officially sponsored programme in the First Five-Year Plan as early as 1951. The problem is indeed gigantic in dimension and intricate in its manifestations, impinging on the social, economic and psychological structure of the nation and the individual at the same time. Though the awareness of the population problem was born in India even during the 1930s, family planning as a national programme was introduced only in 1951.

The essential point to note is that, during 1951-61, the period of the first two Five-Year Plans, emphasis was on "clinical approach", by which people were expected to visit the clinics to avail themselves of family planning advice and services. The experience of the 1951-61 decade taught that, if family planning had to make any headway among the public, it was most essential to take the advice and services to their doorstep. A switchover to the "extension approach" was therefore made in 1963. According to the latest strategy, the programme aims at promoting voluntary acceptance by individuals of one or more methods or devices of contraception through process of education and motivation. To communicate with the individual, a variety of social and psychological barriers surrounding the customs, traditions and practices have to be circumvented.

At the eighth Indian Conference on Family Welfare and Voluntary Sterilisation, held at Cuttack in September 1990, it was disclosed that an estimated 140 million couples in the world are presently depending upon voluntary surgical contraceptives to prevent child birth, accounting for more than 60 per cent of old present users. Currently, about 5 million sterilisations are performed annually in India, and it is expected that this figure is likely to increase to 7 million by 1990-1991.[1]

Another report from New Delhi says that over one million sterilisations were performed from April to August (5 months) in 1990. Kerala (128.4 per cent), Tamil Nadu (122.7 per cent), and Karnataka (110.0 per cent) achieved over 100 per cent of the proportionate targets. Besides, the achievement level in Maharashtra (93.2 per cent), Haryana (88.2 per cent), Andhra Pradesh (82.7 per cent), Punjab (75.2 per cent), and Gujarat (65 per cent) was also higher than the all-India average of 62.0 per cent during the period.

The number of IUD insertions has been 1.39 million. Gujarat, Orissa, Assam, Maharashtra, Kerala, West Bengal, and Tamil Nadu recorded increased performance. During the same period, a total of 5.43 million expectant mothers were covered under tetanus immunisation, and 5.6 million children were immunised against DPT in the country. In addition, 5.67 million children were immunised against polio, 6.49 million against BCG, and 4.87 million against measles. Besides, 1.79 million children were also immunised with DT vaccine, 1.23 million children of 10 years, and 8,74,000 children of 16 years, with TT.[2]

According to Rotary International sources in Washington, a massive India-wide immunisation campaign, costing $ 230 million, was launched in early October to fight several childhood diseases during the campaign organised by Rotary International and other non-Government agencies, along with the Indian Government.

---

1. "Sterilisation Widely Used", *The Statesman*, New Delhi, 25 September, 1990, p. 5.
2. "One Million Sterilisations in 5 Months", *The Statesman*, New Delhi, 24 October, 1990, p. 5.

As many as 1,00,000 Rotarians were expected to work with the Indian Medical Association, UNICEF, and Indian officials on 2 October, 1990, 4 November 1990, and 2 December 1990 for the success of the campaign. Besides, at thousands of medical clinics in 27 States and Union Territories of India, Rotary will provide polio vaccine and tens of thousands of volunteers for the Polio-plus campaign.

Polio-plus is committed to global eradication of polio by the turn of the century. The "plus" represents efforts to combat other childhood diseases. Polio-plus has already committed $ 20 million for immunisation efforts in India, where 44 per cent of the world's cases of polio are reported. The goal of the new *shishu suraksha divas* (baby protection day) is to increase polio coverage from 75 per cent to 85 per cent, thus breaking the transmission of polio. Only one other disease, small-pox, has so far been eradicated.[3]

Can more incentives by Government boost the family planning programme ?

The move to abolish cash incentives for promoters and State Governments, who fulfil family planning targets, is by no means the first indication that our planners have not yet woken up to the dangers posed by India's runaway population growth. This is not necessarily to support the payments system, but to suggest that there is not much evidence as yet of a viable alternative. Much of the success that the family planning programme achieved in the early years was undone, first, by an excess of zeal during the Emergency and, secondly, by a timid Janta Party that was so nervous of alienating voters in the Hindi belt that one of its first actions after coming to power in 1977 was to rename the department as family welfare, and then follow this up with mindless steps that further wrecked the programme.

---

3. "Immunisation Campaign for India", *The Statesman*, New Delhi, 24 September, 1990, p. 6.

Since then, successive Governments at the Centre have shirked taking hard decisions, the emphasis being more on fulfilling assigned quotas rather then introducing a long-term strategy to bring down the rate of population growth by the turn of the century. Tragically, the lure of money and awards only induced individuals and State Governments to advance false claims, so that the statistical achievement of the couple protection rate increasing from 32.1 per cent in 1987 to 41.7 per cent in 1989 meant no corresponding decrease in the birth rate which stands at an alarming 31.3 per thousand.

In view of this sorry neglect of family planning over successive Plan periods, despite the fact that India was the first country to accept an official programme to control numbers, the concern expressed by the authors of the Eighth Plan is a welcome change. The long-awaited shift from a target-oriented programme may yield lasting results, while the funds earlier earmarked for cash incentives should be reallocated to strengthen the infrastructure at the grassroot level. With the right programme and the will to implement it, the Government should not find it difficult to achieve the suggested growth rate of 21 per thousand. But all this can still be undone by politicians who are strongly opposed to the suggestion of a system of disincentives. In fact, the National Front manifesto referred to both incentives and disincentives, while outlining its commitment to family planning, but it now appears that there are few supporters for disincentives within the ruling coalition.[4]

A correspondent points out that the scheme for giving incentives to those who have small families is not rational. A Group "A" Central Government official adopting the norm at the age of 35 will, under the present scheme, get personal pay at Rs. 100 a month for 23 years (till superannuation), besides a half per cent rebate on house-building advance. He may also enjoy special casual leave for 6 working days (14 days in the case of women) for undergoing sterilisation. All this is in addition to the incentives he or she may enjoy at par with any non-

4. "Dangers of Numbers", Second Editorial, *The Statesman*, New Delhi, 24 September, 1990, p. 6.

official. The latter has to be content with Rs. 165. The correspondent asks, "Why this disparity ?"

The scheme, the correspondent says, should be scrapped. Instead of giving cash incentives to those who are considered enlightened, people should be educated. Cash incentives, if at all given to Government officials, should be limited to the lowest rung only.[5]

There is a good deal of truth in what the correspondent says. The slum citizens belong to the lower rung of the social ladder, and therefore cash incentives for them must not be scrapped at present. Meanwhile, education regarding population, family planning, and family welfare must be intensified among these people to promote the small family norm. In order to find out what they thought on the subject, we asked the slum residents the straightforward question, "Can more incentives by Government boost the family planning programme ?" Their responses are represented in Table 47.

Table 47

QUESTION : CAN MORE INCENTIVES BY GOVERNMENT BOOST THE FAMILY PLANNING PROGRAMME ?

Response	*Respondents*	*Percentage*	*Ranking*
Yes	189	63.0	1
No	4	1.3	2
Non-acceptors	107	35.7	—
Total	300	100	—

The table shows that the overwhelming majority of 63 per cent slum residents are in favour of incentives. This is understandable in the context of their generally lower economic status, the prevalence of illiteracy, and their poor living conditions. If the

5. G. Pushkaran, "Small Family", Letter to the Editor, *The Statesman*, New Delhi, 27 September, 1990, p. 6.

saying "money makes the mare go" is to be believed, it must be acted upon, and the amount of incentives—in cash or in kind—must be such as to generate a feeling among the slum residents that the rewards are worth going in for.

Only a negligible minority of 1.3 per cent slum families reported that they needed no incentives, because they were aware of the need for family planning in the context of their own socio-economic constraints. While agreeing with their right thinking, one cannot but point out that the proportion of such people that think on the right lines is shockingly low—only 1.3 per cent in the sample. This calls for greater effort on the part of family planning educators to step up their campaign to raise the proportion of 1.3 per cent to a much higher level, which would be a more convincing testimony to the family planning programme than the mere fulfilment of annual targets.

Should Government impose a fine on the birth of the third and subsequent child ?

A fine on the birth of the third and subsequent child can be imposed with impunity under a ruthless dictatorship. In China, for example, there are deterrent disincentives for those couples who choose to have a second child. But in a country where vote-banks are more important than the interest of the society, it is simply out of the question for any Government even to dream (not to speak of enacting legislation) of levying any fine, however insignificant, on the birth of any number of children, let alone the third or the subsequent child.

One of the many other reasons why Indira Gandhi and her party lost the elections in 1977, paving the way for the Janta Government, was that family planning was made compulsory during the Emergency declared by Indira Gandhi in 1975. Family planning was a purely voluntary affair in the pre-Emergency era, and it still continues to be so after the end of the Emergency; that is, in place of coercion, persuasion is adopted, though the former method yields quicker results, while the latter is a slow-moving process.

Since repressive measures are resented, it is better that people are educated on the gravity of the population problem, on the advantages of planned parenthood, and on the benefits of family health. The understanding should be the outcome of viewing the problem not only from the angle of a population-growing society and the ongoing developmental Work throughout the length and breadth of the country but also from one's own family angle, establishing the correlative between the two angles of vision, so that adequate development benefits filter down to one's progeny.

Table 48 presents the responses of the interviewees to the query wether Government should impose a fine on the birth of the third and subsequent child.

Table 48

QUESTION : SHOULD GOVERNMENT IMPOSE A FINE ON THE BIRTH OF THE THIRD AND SUBSEQUENT CHILD ?

Responses	*Respondents*	*Percentage*	*Ranking*
Yes	2	0.7	2
No	141	63.6	1
Non-acceptors	107	35.7	—
Total	300	100	—

Source : Personal Investigation.

The table reveals that the majority of 63.6 per cent slum respondents prefer the democratic method of voluntary family planning, attracting people through persuasion and publicity, so that the urge for planned parenthood comes from within, and does not turn into a command in a dictatorial manner. They therefore reject the idea that Government should impose a fine on the birth of the third and subsequent child.

The fractional minority of 0.7 per cent slum respondents favour the imposition of fine on those couples who beget a third child or more. These hardliners are impatient of the tardy process of democratic motivation and, afraid of the peril of population explosion looming large on the demographic horizon of India, want quicker results by favouring compulsory family planning after the second child, irrespective of the fact that it smacks of unabashed authoritarianism an unmindful that people would resent and resist it.

A number of family planning devices are at hand, such as (i) Nirodh and vasectomy for men, and (ii) Mala, Copper T, tubectomy, and medical termination of unwanted pregnancy for women. These should be accompanied by medical facilities to supervise their use and also post-use advice and help. The need to educate people in the use of birth control devices, and to propagate them among the slums, is of utmost importance. Simultaneously, there is the need for creating a favourable climate for married couples to accept these devices. This is not easy task, as it involves a big change in their attitude towards the family.

Once family planning acquires social respectability, it will become easier to propagate the use of birth control devices. The publication of material on family planning, the use of radio and television, disseminating information on the occasion of rural festivals, and the like, are to be undertaken to make available to the people knowledge about different contraceptive devices. But such knowledge alone is not sufficient : what is important is that these devices are used by the slum families. The devices should be distributed free to the slum section of the society.

Additional incentives for boosting sterilisation

The re-structured 20-Point Programme includes health for all and the 2-child norm. The Medical Termination of Pregnancy (MTP) Act came into force with effect from 1 April, 1972. It provides for the termination of pregnancy on certain grounds by registered medical practitioners in well-equipped institutions.

There are some cash incentives for sterilisation. For example, a man undergoing vasectomy gets Rs. 200 plus Rs. 10 for diet and Rs. 15 for conveyance, that is, a total of Rs. 235. A woman undergoing tubectomy is given Rs. 125 plus Rs. 30 for diet and Rs. 15 for conveyance, that is, a total of Rs. 170 in all. Needless to say, that these rates need revision upwards, because of rising prices. Lottery awards are also provided—Rs. 10,000 for first prize, Rs, 5,000 as second prize, Rs. 2,000 as third prize, and Rs. 1,000 as fourth prize.

Some States provide additional incentives to couples with a green card, which is issued to those who have undergone sterilisation after 2 or 3 children. These additional incentives include facilities of various types such as free treatment in Government hospitals to the couple and children not above 3 years of age, relaxation of 2 years in the age-limit for entering State Government services, 5 per cent grace marks in examinations, preference in Government jobs, in allotment of residential units, in loans for self-employment, free education in medical and engineering colleges. These supplementary benefits vary from State to State.

During our interview with the slum families in urban Hoshangabad, we found that their ambition was restricted to the achievement of a few modest goals. As the majority of them were engaged in petty business, some of them were interested in securing soft loans to sustain or expand their business. Those who were Government or semi-Government employees were attracted to the principle of time-bound promotions and, along with some other slum-dwellers, desired to shift to a better locality where they could obtain priority in the allotment of residential plots or Government houses.

We put to them the question as to which among the additional incentives, in their opinion, would boost sterilisation in the slum areas. Their responses are recorded in Table 49.

Table 49

QUESTION : SHOULD GOVERNMENT GIVE THE FOLLOWING ADDITIONAL INCENTIVES TO BOOST SURGICAL OPERATIONS FOR FAMILY PLANNING—(I) PRIORITY IN THE ALLOTMENT OF PLOTS AND HOUSES, (II) TIME-SCALE PROMOTION FOR EMPLOYEES, AND (III) LIBERAL LOANS FROM BANKS FOR BUSINESS ?

Additional incentives	*Respondents*	*Percentage*	*Ranking*
Priority in allotment of plots and houses	23	7.7	2
Time-scale promotion for employees	14	4.6	3
Liberal loans from banks for business	156	52.0	1
Non-acceptors	107	35.7	—
Total	300	100	—

Source : Personal Investigation.

According to the table, the top rank (52.0 per cent) goes to those slum families adopting family planning measures who believe that liberal loans from banks for business and agricultural activities will go a long way in bringing a larger number of slum individuals to the operation table. These persons obviously represent those who feel difficulty in obtaining loans from banks with personal efforts and/or those to whom the sum loaned is insufficient for the kind of business/agricultural operations they envisage.

The second place (7.7 per cent) is occupied by those family planning acceptors who hold the view that priority in allotment of residential plots and Government housing would be a sufficient inducement to help the needy slum families to volunteer themselves for vasectomy and tubectomy. Some of these persons were low-paid servants of the Central and State Government or semi-Government organisations who had not been allotted Government accommodation till the time the survey was undertaken, presumably on account of the paucity of Government-owned houses in proportion to the number of Government/semi-Government employees, and had therefore to continue to live in slums. These persons, together with those who wanted a residential plot, wished to shift to a better neighbourhood so as to keep their children away from the slum environment.

The bottom place in the table (4.6 per cent) is relegated to those slum residents who feel that time-scale promotions will attract other employees to the terminal methods of family planning. Apparently, these interviewees are also Government/semi-Government employees who, impatient of having to wait for the long time it takes promotion to fall due in the ordinary course of time, long for time-bound promotions so as to enjoy higher pay and pay-scale till their superannuation. The benefits arising from time-bound promotions would not only uplift their economic status but also their social status, besides helping them to fulfil some of their family liabilities.

Taken together, all the three additional incentives may be taken up on an experimental basis for a couple of years, since they are not only manageable but also do not impose any great burden on the exchequer; and, if the results are encouraging, these measures may be continued, otherwise they may be reviewed or totally withdrawn.

Factors behind increase in numbers

India with a population of 711 million (1982) is the second most populous country in the world. China tops the list with more than 750 million people. India is seventh in land areas, i.e., 2.4 per cent of the world's total land area and supporting 15.5 per cent of the world's population. India's population has been steadily increasing since 1921. The year 1921 is called the "big divide", because after 1921 India's population began to increase sharply. High birth rates were probably matched by near-high death rates before this period.

Since 1921, the fertility and mortality patterns of the population began to vary considerably. Beginning from this decade, the Government became better organised and was able to grapple effectively with the problems of drought, floods, and food scarcity. It undertake suitable measures for epidemic control and treatment of common diseases, thereby avoiding calamities on a national scale. After 1921, India's population became quasistable with a declining mortality and a stationary or slowly declining fertility, resulting in an ever-increasing widening of the demographic gap.

In brief, India's population increased from 236 million in 1891 to 251 million in 1921—only a 15 million increase in 30 years because of famines, epidemics, and the worldwide influenza epidemic of 1918-19. But the 1981 Census showed that India's population grew by 137 million between 1971 and 1981, as against 109 million during the previous decade. After independence, the population of India has almost doubled. It was 347 million in 1947.

India's population is increasing at the rate of 13.6 million per year, which is only a little less than the entire population of Australia (14.8 million), which is 2.5 times the size of India. If the current annual growth rate of 2.5 per cent continues unchecked, the population of India at the turn of the century may well reach one billion.

What are the factors behind the great increase in numbers during the last half century ?

(i) To begin with, India had a large population and even a small and nominal rate of increase would have yielded an impressive addition decade after decade.

(ii) The country's population is increasing fast due to high birth rate and rapidly declining death rate.

(iii) The universality of the married state in India also contributes to the growth of population. Marriage is not only a necessary social institution but also a quasi-religious duty.

(iv) Early marriages still prevail, though most child marriages have disappeared.

(v) The social ban on widow remarriage is gradually disappearing with modernisation which negates the traditional custom of banning widow remarriage. Widow remarriage contributes its small share to the population problem. In the years to come, it is possible that this "social infertility" may altogether disappear from Indian society.

(vi) As long as India continues to be predominantly an agrarian economy, based on traditional unmechanised subsistence agriculture, the need for a large labour force will continue to exist. Due to this need, there is a fixed social and cultural attitude which favours the desire for sons.

(vii) Further, the fact that there are neither old age nor retirement benefits nor any kind of social security for the vast agricultural population bolsters the strong desire for sons who would grow up and not only support the parents in their old age but also survive and succeed to the farmstead.

(viii) Another factor is the beginning of the health revolution in India : perhaps the major decisive factor behind the growth of India's population is the decline of the nation's death rate.

(ix) There is also the development of better communication and transportation, enabling the rapid movement of food and the import of foodgrains from friendly countries which has prevented famine conditions and facilitated improvement of general living conditions. Governmental and political stability in India is also responsible for India's population growth.

(x) The last contributory factor to the growth of India's population has been the absence of any effective widespread family planning, particularly among the rural population. If current levels of fertility and mortality continue and the annual rate of growth hovers round 2.5 per cent, India's population can reach a billion people, or a little less, by 2000 A.D.

Chapter IX

OPINIONS AND ATTITUDES

Today, the population problem is like Frankenstein, a tormenting monster, who brings us disaster in the form of economic setbacks, widespread poverty, and mass unemployment. As a social problem, it presents a condition affecting significant numbers of people in ways considered undesirable, about which it is felt something can be done through collective action. Recognising that a rapidly growing population would be more a hindrance than a help in raising the standard of living of the people, family planning as an official programme was initiated in the early 1950s.

The change in the name of the programme from family planning to family welfare is a reflaction of the Government's anxiety to promote the total welfare of the family and the society. The intention is to take the programme forward in the real sense as an investment in man, by man, and for man. In this task, there is no room of compulsion, coercion, or pressure. The approach is educational and wholly voluntary.

The family welfare programme in India includes (i) educational programme under functional literacy, adult education, and education of the handicapped, (ii) socio-economic development covering welfare of destitute women and children as well as integrated child development services, (iii) health programmes such as universal immunisation, creches for children, and centres for working mothers, and (iv) family planning programme including not only motivation but also distribution of contraceptive devices, sterilisation, and medical termination of pregnancy. Family functions—biological, psychological, social, socialisation—can be performed properly when we have a small family in which proper care and guidance is given to every member of the family.

In India, religion and other cultural diversities have contributed to definite fertility differences. The Hindu tradition, for example, demands that every family should have a son. The traditional Hindu blessing to an Indian bride is, "may you be the mother of eight sons!" A Hindu is expected to adhere to four major goals in his life, namely, *dharma, artha, kama,* and *moksha.* In adhering to these four states of life, the Hindu was expected to adjust his life-patterns suitably. Today, however, most Hindus do not follow the four stages of the Hindu way of life.

Muslims form the second largest community in India. The country came into contact with Islam more than twelve hundred and fifty years ago. Indian Muslims have proved to be both an asset and a liability to this country. It is generally taken for granted that Muslims had poor participation in the earlier days of British rule. But now all this has changed, and the Muslim of today is more receptive and more responsive to modern social, economic, political, scientific and technological changes than his counterpart of yester years.

The main factors which act as obstacles in the family welfare programmes are several and varied : poverty, illiteracy, religious taboos, social inhibitions, general backwardness, casteism, and the like. Religious taboos against birth control do not allow any preventive measure to be used by men or women. Besides, very few fully equipped health centres have been set up, which are not enough to fulfil the needs of the sick and ailing people, Similarly, adequate care is not given to the mother and child in a large family, because parents of too many children are unable to pay attention to every child. Health is a state of complete physical, mental, and social well-being, not merely the absence of disease or infirmity. It is a product of many factors—genetic, heredity, economic status, life style, nutrition, accidental and environmental hazards, and medical care. It is not consistent with our sense of national dignity that we should go on producing children and expecting other nations to feed them.

Choice of methods to attract more people to family planning

Incentives and social work must go together. Social work includes unabated official family planning and family welfare campaigns and also similar activities of voluntary social organisations consistently performed and pursued. Restrictions are obviously disincentives or deterrents or penalties operative against those who do not listen to reason and indulge in indiscriminate reproduction : these ignorant persons harm their own families as well as offset the benefits of development works completed throughout the country. a totalitarian society permits penal measures and achieves quicker results, while in democratic societies such steps are regarded as repressive and politicians oppose them because of the fear of loss of votes.

We, therefore, asked the slum families of urban Hoshangabad the question as to whether, in their judgment, which of the several methods would attract more people to family planning—incentives plus social work or restrictions. Their replies are listed in Table 50.

The table reveals that the majority of 63.0 per cent slum families are in favour of incentives coupled with social work. The slum population is largely illiterate or quasi-literate and slow to react to non-traditional ideas. Hence constant dinning into their ears what they should do, supported by irrefutable proof of

Table 50

QUESTION : BY WHICH OF THE FOLLOWING METHODS WILL MORE PEOPLE BE ATTRACTED TO FAMILY PLANNING—INCENTIVES AND SOCIAL WORK OR RESTRICTIONS ?

Method	*Respondents*	*Percentage*	*Ranking*
Incentives and social work	189	63.0	1
Restrictions	4	1.3	2
Non-acceptors	107	35.7	—
Total	300	100	—

Source : Personal Investigation.

the favourable results achieved by those who had already adopted family planning, would bring conviction among them regarding the merits of family planning. But the results of family planning cannot be so easily demonstrated as, for example, the use of high-yielding varieties of seeds, chemical fertilisers and pesticides, and improved farm machinery, can be shown to farmers to convince them. While the benefits of improved farming methods are evident from a single crop, the advantages accruing to a family on adoption of family planning take a very long time to come up to the surface.

The almost negligible minority of 1.3 per cent of hardcore slum residents insist that, unless stringent measures are imposed, it will take several decades to achieve the optimum level of population growth in India. This shows that this group, though tiny, has done some hard thinking on the subject. Yet, as mentioned earlier, oppressive measures are revolting to, and therefore inappropriate for, members of a non-totalitarian society.

Can family size be planned ?

The vigorous publicity which the national family programme has received throughout every nook and corner of the country has made an overwhelming majority of educated urban population conscious of the need for planned parenthood, but the response is not so overwhelming in slum areas where the majority of economically, socially, and educationally backward sections of society live. Even personal hardships endured by some slum parents with more children than they could afford have not made them realise that they had committed a mistake beyond rectification. They hardly realise that the staggering cost of living today has eroded family incomes, the adverse effect of which is acutely felt by families having many children to feed, to clothe, to give them a good start in life.

While interviewing our respondents, we wanted to ascertain (i) what their attitude to family planning was, (ii) whether they practised family planning, and (iii) whether they were convinced that, with the aid of fertility control devices, others could also plan the size of their family. The responses we obtained are summarised in Table 51.

Table 51

QUESTION : DO YOU BELIEVE THAT FAMILY SIZE CAN BE PLANNED ?

Response	*Respondents*	*Percentage*	*Ranking*
Yes	193	63.0	1
No	00	00.0	2
Non-acceptors	107	35.7	—
Total	300	100	—

Source : Personal Investigation.

The table reveals that the substantial majority of 63.0 per cent slum families in urban Hoshangabad in the sample have a positive attitude towards the limitation of family size. The comparatively better educated among them are aware of the advantages of planned parenthood not only from their personal experience but also from the larger standpoint of population control though some of them were more concerned with the personal benefits likely to accrue from family limitation.

Among the non-acceptors of family planning, some slum

families reported that they were not sure that they could plan their family. A few women had reservations whether they would be permitted by their husbands or in-laws to do so. The orthodox among the slum residents betrayed a negative attitude because they still clung to the "children are a gift of God" theory.

Any objection if children adopt family planning methods after marriage ?

Those who have understood family planning and practise it satisfactorily are expected to appreciate their children adopting family planning methods after marriage, because parents desire that the living standard of their married children should not go down. Similarly, those who are against family planning today may change their thinking tomorrow when the ruthless realities of life hammer them hard. It is therefore likely that the rigidity of some these anti-family planners may relex when their children come of age and marry, and they may not oppose their married children making use of family planning devices. All these are, however, just assumptions : what will exactly happen, only time will tell.

Table 52 indicates the attitudinal direction of the slum families under survey as to whether they have any objection to the adoption of fertility control devices on the part of their children after their marriage.

Table 52

QUESTION : DO YOU HAVE ANY OBJECTION IF YOUR CHILDREN ADOPT FAMILY PLANNING METHODS AFTER MARRIAGE ?

Any objection ?	*Respondents*	*Percentage*	*Ranking*
Yes	202	67.3	1
No	98	32.7	2
Total	300	100	—

Source : Personal Investigation.

As compared to the responses in the previous table (Table 52), the answers of the slum families of urban Hoshangabad in the present table show a slightly upward trend in favour of family planning in terms of the future course of their children. In the earlier table, 63.0 per cent slum families believed that the size of the family could be and should be planned. In the present table, the percentage of those who would like their married children to take up family planning rises to 67.3, showing an increase of 3.0 per cent.

These statistical figures suggest that, among the non-acceptors, a small proportion of 3.0 per cent have come to feel that, while they do not favour family planning in their own case, they would raise no objection if their children, after marriage, adopted family planning measures. This reduces the percentage of hard-liners from 35.7 to 32.7. Who knows that, with the passage of time, there might be a further change for the better in their attitude as well as in the attitude of their children when they marry.

Initiative in family planning

Initiative in adopting family planning in slum areas is as difficult as it was for the mice "to bell the cat". Initiative comes from self-confidence, and self-confidence comes when one is thoroughly knowledgeable of what one is doing or intends to do. Had the slum residents been endowed with initiative, self-confidence and knowledge, they would not have been in slums. However, to be sure, the investigator asked them, "will you take the initiative in adopting family planning?" Their replies are enumerated in Table 53.

Table 53

HOSHANGABAD SLUMS : INITIATIVE IN FAMILY PLANNING

Initiative	*Respondents*	*Percentage*	*Ranking*
Yes	193	64.3	1
No	107	35.7	2
Total	300	100	—

Source : Personal Investigation.

The table reveals that 193 or 64.3 per cent slum families, who had adopted family planning , did not do so on their own : they were motivated by others, largely by official family planning programmers, thus showing clearly the lack of initiative. Now that they had been initiated into family planning and had come to know what it was all about, they reported that they were prepared to take the lead. They forgot that these who had undergone family planning surgery needed no further initiative; but they could certainly, if they wanted to, induce others to take the much-needed initiative.

Those using non-terminal methods are now fully prepared to take the first step (i) in changing their present non-terminal method to some other non-terminal method as and when it suits their convenience, or (ii) in switching over from a temporary method to a permanent method as and when necessity arises.

The 107 or 35.7 per cent non-acceptors, still clinging to the obscurantism of their traditions, evidently lack initiative, because of the absence of the motive-force that urges families towards the imperative of family planning under the sordid socio-economic conditions in the slum areas they live in, not to speak of the society at large.

Education regarding family planning and its adoption

The concept of family planning has to be established as a norm of modern life in India. This would lead to the enhancement of family welfare by improving the health of the mother, the care of the child, and the economic stability of the family.The widespread adoption of the small family pattern would, in the national aggregate, assist in bringing about reductions in the birth rate in harmony with a declining death rate. The young men and women of today would be parents tomorrow. Unless they act quickly and effectively to stem this rapid growth, they will be leaving a dreary legacy to their children.

A complex economic challenge faces the parents of tomorrow. Apart from the existing backlog of millions who are unemployed, the excessive growth of population is bringing in new youngsters into the labour market for jobs every year. In the wider context, what is going on is the rapid depletion of our natural resources—land and its fertility, forests, water, fuel, and others. The parents of tomorrow will feel dangerous imbalances in the eco-system in an even more acute form, unless we succeed in promoting rational policies of planned family, planned development, and also planned environment.

We therefore asked the slum families of urban Hoshangabad whether, in their opinion, people were being educated regarding family planning and its adoption. The answers given by respondents are presented in Table 54.

Table 54

Question : Are people being educated regarding family planning and its adoption ?

Response	*Respondents*	*Percentage*	*Ranking*
Yes	193	64.3	1
No	107	35.7	2
Total	300	100	—

Source : Personal Investigation.

The table reveals that 35.7 per cent of the slum families were adamant in not accepting family planning, in spite of all efforts on the part of family planning campaigners and others to persuade them to adopt it. But the majority of 64.3 per cent slum families reported that adequate education was being imparted to people on family planning and its adoption, the evidence of which was that, influenced by that education, they were now planning their families.

On being further questioned about the reasons which prompted them to adopt family planning, the majority of 64.3 slum respondents gave diverse reasons which revealed their personal problems in their own domestic sphere. Most of them (about 22 per cent) said that their worries and anxieties were lessened. This meant that they expected a planned family to give them some mental and emotional relief in the sense that the less the number of children, theoretically speaking, the less the quantitative decrease in worries and anxieties.

Around 13.7 per cent of them said that family planning would help them in the proper upbringing and education of their children. The slum families realised that, with a few children, they would be able to devote greater attention to the upbringing of children and give them education within their limited income than they normally could have given if the number of children were more. Another 13 per cent said that planned parenthood was likely to give the family economic stability and improved standard of living. It is obvious that income, whatever it is, is likely to go longer where there are fewer children than where there are many.

Another slightly larger proportion of 14.3 per cent respondents said that they had taken up family planning for the sake of the better health of the mother and the children. An insignificant minority of only 1.3 per cent better informed respondents perceived a planned family in the wider context of national considerations.

All these responses show that, in planning a family, the slum couples put their own family interest first and foremost, which is by no means wrong. After all, the norm of planned families is a part of the larger goal of national development programmes : the success of one is dependent on the success of the other.

Responsibility of parents in helping their children to develop a favourable attitude towards a small family

The process of growing up means physical, mental, and emotional unfolding and shaping of an individual into a distinct personality. While the physical and mental needs are acknowledged, most of us still go on as if youngsters have no emotional upsurges and sex feelings and that therefore they need no educative measures. The Hindi cinema of today and the cheap Hindi paperbacks available to slum youngsters miseducate them on the emotional and sex aspects of life.

Sex education not only imparts factual knowledge and explains the reproductive system and processes in a simple and scientific way but also involves developing a capacity to work out value systems. Young people need knowledge and education not only about the physical manifestations of the population problem but also about human sexuality and their own reactions, if they are to respond in a constructive way to the challenges facing them in the adult world of tomorrow.

For preserving the health of the mother, the welfare of the children, the economic stability of the family, and the future prospects of the younger generation, it is desirable to adopt the small family norm or not more than 2 children. Education on aspects of human reproduction and functions has relevance for these purposes : it also helps them in building up attitudes of responsibility and mutual help. In a wider sense, the three major aspects of man's adjustment to the biosphere and the fulfilment of his own being are population, development, and environment.

Table 55 reproduces the responses of the slum interviewees to the query whether, in their opinion, parents have a responsibility to help their children to develop a favourable attitude towards a small family.

The involvement of parents in helping their children to develop a favourable attitude towards a small family can be best understood in terms of sex education. But, leaving aside those who do not believe in family planning at all, many of those slum parents who have limited the size of their family by fertility control feel too shy to explain to their grown-up children facts about human reproductive behaviour. Further, many of the slum

Table 55,

QUESTION : DO YOU THINK THAT PARENTS HAVE A RESPONSIBILITY TO HELP THEIR CHILDREN TO DEVELOP A FAVOURABLE ATTITUDE TOWARDS A SMALL FAMILY ?

Response	*Respondents*	*Percentage*	*Ranking*
Yes	202	67.3	1
No	98	32.7	2
Total	300	100	—

Source : Personal Investigation.

parents are themselves largely ignorant of the anatomy of men and women except in some general terms. They therefore confessed that, while they do make attempts through other trustworthy relatives and friends to help their children in adopting a favourable attitude towards a small family, it will be better if this responsibility is taken away from them and entrusted to some institutions for better results.

A handful of educated slum residents argued that sex education must be imparted, simply and scientifically, in the higher classes (XI and XII) of 10 + 2 courses as a part of Social Studies or Biology, as well as in the undergraduate courses in colleges and universities as a part of the Foundation Course, General Knowledge, or General Awareness, whatever be its nomenclature, because even if some parents are knowledgeable they do not possess costly models and charts essential for this purpose. A few respondents had a point when they suggested that 2-week, 3-week, or 4-week condensed courses on sex education should be conducted free twice a year in State hospitals, dispensaries, health centres, and even private maternity and nursing homes for the benefit of young people during Dussehra-Diwali and summer vacations, with the option of attending any one of them according to their convenience.

The youngsters of today who receive such fundamental knowledge will find it more meaningful in personal terms when.

on achieving marriage and parenthood, they have to make important decisions on planning their own families. At certain points, population, education and sex or family-life education converge and have common elements.

If essential knowledge is withheld from the young, because it is new and unconventional, it will mean that millions of young men and women will remain unprepared to face the overwhelming challenge of family life and population growth. It is all the more incumbent that they should be exposed to new ideas and concepts, as early as possible, in forms appropriate to their age-groups and degree of understanding. This applies with special force to aspects where personal attitudes and behaviour are involved.

Polygamy and its purpose

Polygamy is the rule, custom, or condition of marriage to more than one person at a time. It is sometimes confused with polygamy which is the custom, practice, or condition of having a plurality of wives. Polygamy is the basis of mating with more than one female.

Polygamy, in the strict sense of the term, does not exist in the slum areas of Hoshangabad. But there are occasional cases where the divorced or the widowed have married again. There may also be a few clandestine cases of extra-marital relations among the slum residents. As such, if the remarriage of the divorced or separated results in children, and if there are also children born out of wedlock, these have a bearing on population growth and therefore come under the purview of family planning and family welfare.

Wherever polygamy is practised, legitimately or illegitimately, it is due to certain basic reasons such as (i) the quenching of sexual thirst, (ii) the desire for novelty, or (iii) to have a child of there is no issue from the marriage.The reasons given by the 300 respondents comprising of both family planning acceptors and non-acceptors why, in their opinion, polygamy is adopted are delineated in Table 56'.

Table 56
REASONS FOR ADOPTING POLYGAMY

Reasons	*Respondents*	*Percentage*	*Ranking*
Quenching sexual thirst	201	67.0	1
Novelty	95	31.7	2
Having a child	4	1.3	3
Total	300	100	—

Source : Personal Investigation.

The main reasons for adopting polygamy, as reported by the majority of 67.0 per cent slum respondents, is the quenching of sexual thirst. Where the husband comes home too tired or drunk and goes to sleep, or where the husband has been away from home for many months, or where the husband has been ill for a long time, or where the husband is partly or wholly impotent, and the wife is accustomed to cohabitation, and somebody to the wife's liking is easily available to satisfy her sexual appetite, illicit polygamy seems to be the only way out.

A sizeable number of 31.7 per cent respondents affirmed that cohabitation with the same person in the same manner to which he is habituated leads to monotony which can be dispelled by variety and novelty. Some women on the look-out for diversity and newness search for a desirable man about whom there are whispers of variety and longer duration and, if such a person is entrapped under convenient circumstances, polygamy is adopted in a concealed manner. The novelty may arise from the fact that the man comes of a different caste or community and is believed by the woman to be endowed with sexual qualities and behaviour different from those of the woman's husband.

The small minority of only 1.3 per cent slum respondents maintained that a few women desirous of achieving motherhood, who are disappointed in having a child from their lawful husband, tend to gratify their maternal instinct by mating with another man, with or without the consent and connivance of their husbands, in order to conceive a child who, when delivered, passes off for all practical purposes as the legitimate child of the married couple.

There seems to be a good deal of truth in what the slum respondents reported, but the investigator did not come across specific cases of polygamy in the slum areas surveyed by her. What was said by the respondents was little else than hypothetical and could not be corroborated by concrete evidence.

Should the system of polygamy be changed ?

The system of polygamy, as stated earlier, does not exist in the slum areas of Hoshangabad, though an occasional near-polygamous illicit relation may be there. Polygamy, in this sense, amounts to promiscuous relations on the part of women. Such relations do not have the sanction of the slum elders. The Hindus, the Muslims, and the Christians inhabiting the Hoshangabad slums are all monogamous and frown even upon bigamy. They expect the wife and the husband to be loyal to each other, though conjugal fidelity is sometimes breached by an occasional but concealed lapse on the part of a few men and women.

The answers of 300 slum respondents to the question whether they felt that the system of polygamy must be changed are recorded in Table 57.

While denying the prevalence of polygamy in their residential areas, the majority of 99.3 per cent slum respondents reported that wherever the system of polygamy prevailed, it must be changed as it was pernicious. The very idea of a woman having more than one husband is revolting. The case of Draupadi in *The Mahabharat*, they said, was an exception, and they would not like to comment on it. In their opinion, the ideal form of marriage is monogamy, because it elevates the status of a woman as a human being, consistent with reason and dignity, from the lower level of a female animal mating with several male animals when under heat, prompted by instinct and lack of reason. If every woman were to be polygamous, the entire social order, at its present evolutionary stage, would disintegrate.

Table 57

SHOULD POLYGAMY SYSTEM BE CHANGED ?

Response	*Respondents*	*Percentage*	*Ranking*
Yes	298	99.3	1
No	2	0.7	2
Total	300	100	—

Source : Personal Investigation.

The fractional minority of only 0.7 per cent slum respondents said that, while they were against the system of polygamy,they would not like to deny a woman the fulfilment of her motherhood when the fault lay not in herself but in her husband, and divorce was neither desirable nor possible under their circumstances. In such a case, if the woman has a child from another man, the whole affair being hush-hush, and both husband and wife are happy with the child, they would not raise their eyebrows in disapproval. Such cases, it seems to the investigator, are almost similar to the "test tube babies" in USA where an ovum fertilised by the sperm of some other man in injected into the ovary of a child-bearing woman.

Favouring widow re-marriage

The proportion of widowers and widows in the sample survey is minimal—only 5 or 1.3 per cent (vide Table 17). Out of these five, 3 are widows and 2 are widowers. The percentage of widows thus works out to only one per cent in the sample. If a widow is young and issueless, her remarriage poses fewer problems. But if she is middle-aged and has children, only an older widower with children might agree to marry her, while being haunted by the constant anxiety how the children of both would fare in such matrimony. If a widow is self-supporting, she may not care to re-marry on account of the same anxiety about her child/children. If the widower is rich, even young virgins would be urged to marry him, even though he has children by the deceased wife.

There are, however, still some orthodox families with closed minds, even in slums, who believe that "once a widow, always a widow". The foundation of this belief is the dubious argument that once a woman is tied in matrimony it is her religious duty to owe allegiance to her man as long as he is alive, and to his *memory* when he predeceases her. This argument based on the inequality of the sexes, carried to its extreme, would even justify *sati* or the immolation of the widow on the funeral pyre of her husband, although the interviewees did not say so in clear terms.

The replies of the 300 interviewees in the sample survey to the question whether they were in favour of widow remarriage are given in Table 58.

Table 58

QUESTION : ARE YOU IN FAVOUR OF WIDOW REMARRIAGE ?

Response	*Respondents*	*Percentage*	*Ranking*
Yes	297	99.0	1
No	3	1.0	2
Total	300	100	—

Source : Personal Investigation.

The table reveals that the largest majority of 99 per cent slum families favour widow remarriage, irrespective of whether the widow is young or not, self-supporting or dependent, issueless or with children. The reasons generally assigned are that, in re-marrying (i) the widow finds another life-partner to replace the one she has lost for ever; (ii) that her children, if any, find a foster father, (iii) that, if she is without any means of livelihood, the new husband will provide her with at least food, clothes, and shelter: (iv) that, if there is love and companionship between the two, the woman will not feel isolated and lonely and will have someone to care for her as she cares for him; (v) that a widow's life is a void which can be filled up only by remarriage, and (vi) that re-marriage brings back to the widow the glow and respectability of married life which effaces from her the social stigma of being a widow.

A negligible minority of only one per cent respondents were hostile to widow re-marriage. They said they had been told that re-marriage of widows had been banned for several centuries, and that some men imbued with new fangled ideas advocated widow re-marriage. (The reference is perhaps to the enlightened Bengali reformers like Ishwar Chander Vidyasagar and those who followed his footsteps and who were staunch champions of the re-marriage of widows). They further said that a widow was an inauspicious being, who brings bad luck to people, and for this reason she is deprived of many good things of life.

Should parents explain the facts of life to their children ?

Discoveries in the field of science and medicine have led man to acquire control over death to an unprecedented extent. By the same way, he can also control birth and family size, so that the procreative functions are not left to blind chance. Due to age-old habits and sentiments, measures to control death were invested with an aura of humanitarianism, but the regulation of birth was wrongly regarded as being hedonistic. It was realised much later that it formed an essential part in the totality of the process of birth and death. The rampant growth of population compelled people to recognise the urgent need for promoting birth control.

Spacing and limiting the number of children is one of the major factors in promoting family welfare. Not only can parents give better care and attention to their children thereby, but the marital relationship can also be strengthened through the flowering of the expression of mutual love and consideration for each other—a situation which hardly exists where woman is treated as a child-bearing machine and man as the patriarch retaining an upper hand over the whole family.

Some of the objectives underlying the need for parents to explain the facts of life to their children are :

(i) creating among the younger generation an understanding of the rapid growth of population, its causes, trends, factors affecting its growth, and ways of regulating it;

(ii) studying the influence of population trends on the various aspects of life, namely, social, cultural, economic, political and, in particular, the close interaction of population growth and the developmental process with special reference to the national programme to raise the standards of living;

(iii) recognising the fact that scientific developments are enabling us to get increasing control over famine, disease, and untimely death, as well as control over unplanned births, and that this body of knowledge has to be utilised to correct violent imbalances between the two in order to create stability;

(iv) realising the significance of population growth on the individual and on his family life, and encouraging attitudes of responsibility, mutual help, and cooperation in all aspects of personal and family living; and

(v) appreciating the fact that for preserving the health of the mother, the welfare of the children, and the future prospects of the younger generation, our families today and in the future should be small and compact with no more than one or two children.

The investigator briefly discussed the major points of the need for parents to explain the facts of life to their children with the slum residents of urban Hoshangabad and discovered that many of them knew something about the points covered. Having assured herself of having enabled the interviewees to answer her query in the right perspective, she asked them whether parents should explain these facts of life to their children. Their answers are presented in Table 59.

Table 59

QUESTION : SHOULD PARENTS EXPLAIN THE FACTS OF LIFE TO THEIR CHILDREN ?

Response	*Respondents*	*Percentage*	*Ranking*
Yes	202	67.3	1
No	98	32.7	2
Total	300	100	—

Source : Personal Investigation.

The table reveals that the majority of 67.3 per cent respondents were of the view that facts of life must be explained to their children, but the obligation to do so must fall not only on parents but also on educational institutions, voluntary organisations, specially on family planning programmers who should conduct short-duration courses for boys and girls emerging out of their adoescence in the context of prevailing socio-economic scenario.

A sizeable proportion of 32.7 per cent slum respondents said that they did not relish the idea of parents explaining the facts of reproduction and family planning methods to their own children, because they thought that (i) it would be a shame to teach children what their own parents had been doing in secret to give them birth, (ii) the parents would thus feel degraded in the eyes of their own children whom they dearly loved, and (iii) the adolescent children are likely to be provoked into making all kinds of sex experiments which would defeat the very purpose of such education, leading them astray.

The fact of the matter is that population and sex education is a flexible subject which may have a place to itself in the school syllabus and/or may be inserted into the curriculum at various points in classes pertaining to such subjects as modern history, economic or human geography, social studies, biology, nature study, Indian economics, hygiene and physiology, and allied subjects.

As a step towards ensuring a hopeful and progressive future for itself, the coming generation must be accorded the opportunity to acquire, in a timely and graded manner, an understanding of this modern phenomenon of burgeoning human population, and the ways it interacts with social, economic, and political aspects of life, influencing not only the physical standards but also the very quality of human living.

Teaching population dynamics should not become a mere recital of facts and figures, leading to a dull and dismal learning by rote. It is a lively subject, deeply concerned with the social order and the endeavour to attain a harmonious equilibrium in resources. The underlying factors and concepts, which contribute to the dynamics of population and its trends, are a significant part of human ecology.

Chapter X

SUMMARY AND CONCLUSION

In our country, as in many other countries, there is hardly a city without any eyesores, and Hoshangabad is no exception. Slums are for those families who do not have the means to pay the high rent of a good house in good locality, not to speak of owning one. Slums are therefore the enforced habitat of families which are economically, socially, and educationally weak. The worst slums comprise of shanties, or make-shift structures of tin sheets, plastic sheets, even old gunny bags, mud or brick walls, without any plan or pattern, and are usually unauthorised structures on encroached Government land.

Each jhuggi or jhonpri measures on an average approximately between 8 and 10 feet in length, and between 6 and 8 feet in breadth, with a roof of tin or plastic sheets at a height varying between 6 and 8 feet. The floor is entirely of mud. The abode has only a single narrow door and no window. Thus it is often damp and dark, with neither flow of air not sunlight. All these factors are most conducive to the growth of disease-bearing bacteria. During her survey of urban Hoshangabad, the writer has identified 9 slum areas for the purpose of the present study. These areas, with varying population in terms of numbers, castes and communities, scattered in different parts of urban Hoshangabad, constitute the universe of study.

Family planning and family welfare

India has the distinction of being the first country in the world to launch a nation-wide family planning programme with full government support. Family planning has, however, to be lifted from its old and narrow concept and given its proper place in the overall programmes of welfare, particularly those which are designed to protect and promote the health of mothers and children. It must become a part of the total concept of positive health. At the same time, it must find meaningful integration with other welfare programmes, namely, nutrition, clothing, shelter, availability of safe drinking water, education, employment, and women's welfare.

Responsible parenthood

The Government attaches the highest importance to the dignity of the citizen and to his right to determine the size of his family. By and large, the people of India are conscious of the importance of responsible parenthood. Given the necessary information and adequate services, they will accept the small family norm. Promotion must be given to all methods with equal emphasis, and it should be left to every family to decide what method of contraception it would like to adopt. Employees of the union Government, State Governments, autonomous bodies, local bodies, and others, are expected to set an example and to adopt the small family norm.

In a federal system, the sharing of Central resources with the States is a matter of considerable importance. Family planning and population is a subject in the concurrent list, yet the implementation of the family welfare programme is very much the responsibility of the Government of India.

Strategy for enlarging family welfare

Family welfare programme, which is an essential part of the strategy of enlarging welfare, is being implemented as a wholly voluntary programme and as an integral part of the overall strategy of growth, covering health, maternity and child care, family welfare, women's rights, and nutrition.

The salient features of the strategy are : (i) intensified efforts to spread awareness and information through imaginative use of multi-media and interpersonal communication, (ii) provision of services and supplies as close to the doorsteps of the acceptors as possible, (iii) development of facilities for rapid increase in female literacy, (iv) population education to the young in schools and colleges as well as those out of schools; (v) assistance and support of the elected representatives of the people, (vi) proper linkages with other Ministries and Departments concerned, (vii) incentives to individual acceptors and State Governments, and (vii) close monitoring and follow-up of the programme at all levels.

Factors affecting the implementation of the family welfare programme

The family welfare programme is an important national programme in the socio-economic planning of the society. This comprehensive national programme emphasises human resource development and improving the quality of life of the people. Despite the recent progress in the implementation of the programme, the desired objectives could not be achieved so far. There is a wide gap between the actual fertility levels and fertility goals laid down by the Government. Diverse social and cultural factors play an important role in the variation in acceptance and non-acceptance of the programme throughout the country. The family, the kinship structure, husband-wife decision-making, values and disvalues of children, and interpersonal communication, affect the implementation of the programme to a considerable extent.

Factors producing change in various aspects of family structure

Economic factors are significant in fertility decisions, both influencing the desire for large families and creating pressures to stop having children. But motivational processes are complex and economic factors do not operate independently of social and emotional considerations. The factors responsible for change in family include social legislation, urbanisation, education, industrialisation, geographical mobility, individualistic values, and contacts with western societies. It is assumed that these factors produce inevitable change in various aspects of family structure. Although the family is the most conservative institution, only next to religion it is not left untouched by the process of modernisation.

Sex ratio

Present-day parents who, due to whatever circumstances, heedlessly continue to have large families are doing a great disservice to their own progeny who, in turn, might deepen the crisis by again repeating the pattern when they themselves become parents, unless they arrive at a full realisation of the truth in good time. The sex ratio in the sample is slightly tilted in favour of women who constitute 52.7 per cent of the 300 slum families taken up for study, as against 47.3 per cent men. In other words, the proportion of women exceeded that of men by 5.4 per cent. This variation may be just coincidence in the sample, or it may be due to the fact that some of the men may have left the slums for employment at places so distant from their home that it is not possible for them to do up and down every day.

It is these slum people of both the sexes, whatever be their sex ratio, upon whom the attention of the family planning programmers should be largely concentrated since they constitute the lowest stratum of urban society. To start educating them about the small family norm when they are already deep set in their ways (and probably have 3 or 4 children) is like starting to dig a well when fire is consuming the house.

Age group

The majority of 40.7 per cent respondents were in the age-group of 21-25 years, followed by 24.7 per cent respondents who were in the age-group of 16-20 years. The later age-group suggests that early marriage is also prevalent among the slum-dwellers of urban Hoshangabad, specially the marriage of teen-age girls. In other words, the couples between the age of 16 and 20 were clamped into a domestic routine, with children to bring up, before they themselves had matured in terms of worldly experience. Had they belonged to a better social stratum, these boys and girls would have been studying in various educational institutions. While 18.7 per cent respondents were between 26 and 30 years, the lesser number of 14.3 per cent respondents were in the 31-40 age-group. The minority of 1.6 per cent respondents in the sample were above 40 years.

Marital status

Ascertaining the marital status of individuals is important in order to study how they respond to the family planning programmes in Hoshangabad slums. If they are married, we come to know what role they have played—successfully, perfunctorily, or none at all—in the planning as well as in the health management of their family. If they are married, interpersonal contact with them helps us in eliciting information whether they have any plans with regard to the size and welfare of the family they will bring up. If one of the spouses has predeceased the other, or is divorced or separated, but still young and hoping to remarry, interviewing such a respondent has a double advantage : we learn from the interviewees what he or she has done with regard to planned parenthoodandfamily health during the first marriage, and what he or she has in mind with regard to this crucial demand of modern existence if he or she marries again.

None of the respondents in the sample was unmarried.The vast majority of 92 per cent respondents were married. The minority of 3.7 per cent respondents were separated, while the almost negligible proportion of 1.7 per cent among the slum-dwellers consisted of either widows or widowers.

Educational status

There is a definite correlation between one's educational attainment and the number of children one tends to have. In general, the higher and wider the level of one's education, the more the skill to understand things in their proper perspective. The responsiveness to the changing situation, with which an individual is perpetually besieged, goes on increasing with each step upward in the educational ladder, and even throughout life.

The largest majority of 75.3 per cent respondents living in the 9 slums of Hoshangabad are illiterate, which seems to be the general characteristic of the slum population not only in Madhya Pradesh but also all over India. The remaining 24.7 per cent of the respondents are unequally distributed in terms of educational levels,. 9.3 per cent of them are literate, perhaps because of the adult literacy drive. by "literate", we mean an individual who knows simple reading and writing but who had no formal education up to the primary level. As the level of education rises, the proportion of respondents decreases, because of drop-outs largely caused by economic necessity.

Occupational status

The minority of 9.7 per cent slum-residents are able to get jobs as petty employees or are self-employed doing less remunerative work, while 10.7 per cent are currently out of work. The largest proportion of 60.3 per cent slum-dwellers earn their daily bread through petty business, working largely as hawkers and pedlars, selling perishable agricultural commodities like vegetables, fruits, fish, eggs, and sometimes trinkets and cheap ornamental articles.

The next largest proportion of 19.3 per cent slum-residents are engaged in agricultural activities—preparing the field, sowing, watering, weeding, harvesting, bundling, threshing, winnowing, packing, and the like. A few have inherited little plots of land, from which they eke out a living. A few others keep one or two buffaloes and sell milk, or keep poultry and sell chicken and eggs. The slum-residents deserve first priority in all family planning and family welfare programme.

Members in the family

With the average monthly income of a slum family, accompanied by mounting inflation throughout the country, it is self-explanatory that a large-size family is comparatively in a tighter situation than a small-size family as regards the basic necessities of life, not to speak of comforts, while luxury is something beyond the dreams of slum-dwellers. The economic, educational, and social backwardness of slum-dwellers, rare exceptions apart, serve almost as strong barriers in climbing up the economic, educational, and social ladder.

The largest proportion of 49.7 per cent slum families have 5 members each, all living together under the same roof. The next largest proportion of 30.7 per cent families have 4 members each which, in general, suggests parents and two children when the survey was undertaken. The minority of 19.6 per cent families have 6 members each, which denotes not only over crowding and absence of privacy in their small residential space but also economic difficulties. The widowed, the divorced, and the separated have a relatively harder time, irrespective of the fact whether their family has less or more members.

Siblings living with the family

Among the 300 slum families surveyed, 261 or 87 per cent families had no siblings living with them. The remaining 39 or 13 per cent families were burdened with 45 siblings, which works out to an average of 1.15 siblings per family. Among these 39 families, 9 families, taken together, had 10 sister/

sisters-in-law living with them, followed by 8 families where the father-in-law resided with them, and then followed by 5 families with brother/brothers-in-law. The least number is that of 3 families which included 4 brothers in all. These statistics show that, owing to their being largely weaker sections of society, only 13 per cent of the slum families in the sample survey are able to keep one or two relatives with them, and not more. The concept of a large joint family therefore cannot be entertained by them on account of economic and housing constraints.

Literacy/education of parents and grandparents

Social change in terms of literacy/education of grandparents and parents of slum children can be statistically measured by the increase between the literacy/education of the two generations : increase showing favourable change, and decrease revealing unfavourable change. As literacy/education of parents has some impact on children, literate/educated parents would also like their children to be literate/educated at least up to, if not higher than, the level of education than they themselves had achieved, which, suggests a movement forward. Illiterates who encourage their children to have some formal education also more in the forward direction. Illiterates who keep their children illiterate like themselves reveal a level of stagnation. Those literates or educated who deny the new educational facilities to their children take a step backwards : they are educationally retrogressive.

As mentioned earlier, out of 300 respondents, 226 or 75.[illegible] per cent were illiterate, while the remaining 74 or 24.7 per cent were literate/educated. There was more literacy among husbands (57 or 19 per cent) than among wives (17 or 6.7 per cent). Similarly, among grandparents, a total of only 44 individuals were literate/educated : the ratio being 36 : 8, that is 36 grandfathers and only 8 grandmothers. The figures reveal a rise in literacy/education in the sample survey : an increase of 30 individuals or 10 per cent (74 literate/educated parents as against only 44 literate/educated grandparents). The highest increase has been in women's literacy/education, which has slightly doubled (17 mothers as against only 8 grandmothers).

Economic status

So long as people remain economically unsound due to employment or underemployment, or earn a deplorably low income, birth control publicity is likely to fall on deaf ears. Slum areas are comparatively less prosperous than non-slum areas. The slow pace of industrialisation in around Hoshangabad has not improved the economic status of its inhabitants as much as that of the salaried or wage-earning class in relatively better industrialised proximate cities like Bhopal, Dewas, or Indore.

The largest proportion of 24.3 per cent among the slum-residents have an income below Rs. 1,000 per month per family, which, in these days of spiralling inflation, suggests that such families are living from hand to mouth and some of them are likely to be indebted. The next highest proportion of 22 per cent slum families have an income varying between Rs. 1,001 and Rs. 1,500 per month, which again presents a bleak situation if the family happens to be a large one.

Those with a family income varying between Rs. 1,501 and Rs. 2,000 per month constitute only 18 per cent in the sample survey which, according to slum standards, indicates a marginally better-off living standard. Another 15 per cent slum families are in subordinate Government service, or in petty business, or are small agriculturists cultivating their ancestral land. The few (10 per cent), whose family income is more than Rs. 2,500 per month, are relatively more prosperous in terms of slum life-style : they have more than one earning member and their total income, pooled together, exceeds Rs. 2,500 per month.

Small savings

The proportion of 10.7 per cent slum residents are unemployed : it is therefore inconceivable that they should save. The monthly income of 24.3 per cent respondents is below Rs. 1,000, and hence saving is beyond their meagre means. Another 22 per cent slum residents earn between Rs. 1,001 and Rs. 1,500 per month which, keeping the ever-increasing inflation in mind, also keeps them out of the saving group. Yet another 18 per cent slum families earn between Rs. 1,501 and Rs. 2,000 per month. These numerically four-figure incomes are again offset by the interminable inflation. Thus, 75 per cent of the total slum residents in the sample are eliminated from the savers.

This leaves 25 per cent respondents : the family income of 15 per cent among them ranges between Rs. 2,000 and Rs. 2,500 per month, while that of 10 per cent families exceeds Rs. 2,500 per mensem. Theoretically, they are expected to save, but the survey shows that, among them, the marginal proportion of 7.7 per cent families are savers, while the economic status of the overwhelming majority of 92.3 per cent slum families is so low that they are in no position to save at all.

Reasons for saving

Whatever allurement publicity for small savings may hold, the naked fact is that there must be some surplus left, after meeting day-to-day expenses, which one may save and, under proper guidance and supervision, invest and re-invest. To expect an average slum-dweller to save is to forget that he is a slum-dweller. Had his income been better, he would not be living in a slum.

The sample reveals that, while it is utterly beyond the capacity of the predominant majority of 277 or 92.3 per cent slum residents to save, only 23 or 7.7 per cent slum residents do save. Among the slender majority of 6.4 per cent savers are employees of government or semi-Government and allied organisations, who are under compulsion to save some money per month on account of statutory deductions from their salary in the form of contributions to provident fund and other schemes for the benefit of these employees. The microscopic minority of 1.3 per cent slum-dwellers invested whatever they saved in the petty business they were engaged in.

Attitude towards family planning

The overwhelming majority of 80.3 per cent slum women favoured birth control, which bears testimony to the extent of family planning awareness aroused among the residents of these sensitive areas that are commonly believed to resist or sidetrack both planned parenthood and measures.

Almost one-fifths (19.7 per cent) told the investigator in unequivocal terms that they were against family planning, because

(i) they were totally ignorant of the basics of family planning;

(ii) as family planning had never been practised in their family, the elders were opposed to it;

(iii) they found themselves to be too timid to talk to their elders about its necessity and its resultant advantages and disadvantages;

(iv) unless their husbands were won over to the concept of family planning, they were helpless and unable to involve themselves in it on their own; and

(v) they themselves were apprehensive of family planning, as it would be something strange and novel for them which might have an adverse effect on their health and family life.

It needs no reiteration that the majority of those who did not favour family planning were absolutely illiterate.

Age at marriage

The survey reveals that the age-old pernicious custom of marrying girls before the age of 18 is still widely in vogue among the largely illiterate and semi-educated families living in the slums of urban Hoshangabad, as evidenced by a fairly large majority of 40.7 per cent girls who were united in wedlock in their tender teens. The hackneyed arguments commonly put forward are :

(i) that girls are *paraya dhan* (the property of the would-be husband's family);

(ii) That they are likely to go astray if they are not married early;

(iii) that, on attaining the age of puberty, they are biologically fit to marry; and

(iv) that it is the sons, and not daughters, who perpetuate the family name.

Another proportion of 40 per cent slum girls were married at an age varying between 18 years and 20 years, and were thus outside the purview of the legislation in respect of the marriage of minors. The minority of 19.3 per cent girls married at an age ranging between 21 years and 25 years, not largely because the slum families favoured late marriages, but mainly because they could not arrange the marriage of their daughter/ daughters earlier.

Wife-husband age difference

Brides younger than grooms by a few years are generally preferred in marriage, although there are rare exceptions where husbands are younger than their wives. In Indian society, the matrimonial preference for girls being rather younger than boys seems to be based on the commonly accepted belief that the tropical climate of the country generally makes women age faster than men in the sense that the bloom of their youth fades away quicker than that of men.

The sample shows that the majority of 68 per cent slum women in urban Hoshangabad were younger by their spouses by the age-group ranging between 3 and 6 years. The next highest proportion of 20.7 per cent slum women were younger than their husbands by less than 3 years. In a few cases (9.3 per cent), the slum wives were younger than their husbands by the age-group varying between 6 and 9 years. The age gap between the spouses rarely extended over 9 years (one per cent) : it was zero when the almost negligible proportion of 0.6 per cent of married partners were of equal age. The broad conclusion is that the general preference in the slums of urban Hoshangabad is that the bride should be younger than the groom by 3, 4, 5, or at the most 6 years.

Surviving children

The sample highlights that the 300 slum families of urban Hoshangabad have a total of 1,153 surviving children. The number of male surviving children (577) almost equals that of female surviving children (576). The average number of surviving children per family works out to 3.84. This includes those families who have only one child (and may want one or two more) and also those who have 2, 3, 4, 5, or 6 children. This calls for more intensive efforts to reduce child births either by terminal or by non-terminal methods, but preferably by means of the former, specially by persuasion coupled with the temptation of incentives.

Place of baby's birth

The sample tells us that the majority of 52 per cent slum families have the child delivered at home, because they are either poor or have no time to take the would-be mother to the Government hospital on account of last-minute labour pains. When the nearest midwife cannot be called instantly, experienced old women in the house or in the proximate neighbourhood substitute for the midwife as a make-shift arrangement.

The next highest proportion of 28.7 per cent slum families take the expectant mother to the Government hospital at Hoshangabad. There is almost cent per cent satisfaction from the maternity services offered by this hospital, where prenatal and postnatal services are also available, including sterilisation facilities.

The minority of 19.3 per cent slum families have the child delivered at the father/mother-in-law's home, especially the first child. It is an open secret that the expenses are borne, not by the husband and his family, but by the wife's family.

Mother's age at the birth or her first child

The sample reveals that the large majority of 70 per cent slum mothers were between 18 and 20 years of age when their first child was born. If they were 18 years of age at the time they begot their first offspring, many of them must have been married when they were legally minors. if they were 20 when they gave birth to their first child, many of them were still teenagers at the time of marriage. A small proportion of 7 per cent mothers, who were below the age of 18, is clear evidence of child marriages. The broad inference, therefore, is that the undesirable custom of the marriage of minors and teenagers is widely prevalent among the slum residents of urban Hoshangabad.

A proportion of 22 per cent mothers delivered their first baby when they were between 21 and 25 years. This suggests either marriage on legally attaining the age of majority of the use of contraceptive devices. The minority of one per cent slum mothers, who had their first child between the age of 26 and 30, either married late or were strict acceptors of family planning. It may also be that either they were suffering from some gynaecological disorder or their husbands were temporary victims of some infirmity in their reproductive behaviour.

Mother's age at the birth of her youngest child

The sample reveals that a large proportion of 41.7 per cent slum mothers were between the age of 21 and 25 when their youngest child was born, followed by 29.2 per cent mothers whose youngest child was born between the age of 26 and 30 years. The proportion of mothers belonging to the youngest age-group of 18-20 years when their youngest child was born works out to 17.7 per cent. The minority of 9.7 per cent mothers were between the age of 31 and 35 years when they gave birth to their youngest child, while the minimal minority of 1.7 per cent mothers had crossed the age of 35 when they begot their youngest offspring.

These statistics suggest that all these age-groups are potential groups where family planning and family welfare education needs to be stepped up. Those mothers who were above 35 need to be reminded that, at their age, if they continue to have children, they would be burdened with additional liabilities and they may grow too old to see their last child settled in life. The norm of a small family, not exceeding one or two children, must be made clear to them because, under the slum conditions in which they are living, they can ill afford to give more children better education and better opportunities in life, unless they are content to turn their children into mere replicas of their own selves. Commonsense demands that their succeeding generation must be better in many respects than they themselves.

Wanting more children

The sample reveals that a small minority of 17.7 per cent slum mothers wanted more children. Most of them were in their early twenties, and many of them had one child which was not enough for them, as they put it. Where their sole child was a son, they wanted a sister for him, and where their only child was a daughter, they desired a brother for her, so that the sex difference could be equalised. A few who had a still birth or a miscarriage wanted a live-born child as a replacement.

But the large majority of 82.3 per cent slum mothers did not want more children, as they felt that they had enough. Most of these mothers were in their late twenties or early thirties. They had come to this conclusion either because of their own personal experience of hardship or because they had been influenced by the country wide publicity commending birth control devices, the benefits of having a small family, and the immunisation of babies and expectant mothers.

Yet there seems to be a snag in their responses : *wanting*

no more children is one thing, *having* no more children quite another. In spite of not wanting, they may have children, unless they adopt terminal measures because, without doing so, "there is many a slip 'twixt the cup and the lip", as the significant saying goes.

Responses for and against family planning

It would be too much to expect 100 per cent family planning in any section of society, least of all in slum areas, so long as family planning remains voluntary. Yet much motivation seems to have been done in bringing the slum residents closer to the acceptance of family planning where they do not have to pay for anything out of their own pockets. That is why the majority of 64.3 per cent residents of urban Hoshangabad adopted family planning.

The proportion of non-acceptors comes to the sizeable percentage of 35.7 (more than one-thirds of the slum families surveyed), and it is these families on whom the family welfarè workers have to concentrate more attention by removing their stock objections or genuine apprehensions through friendly discussion and persuasion in a language the slum families easily understands.

Birth control measures

Slum residents in urban Hoshangabad (with 29 per cent women having undergone tubectomy and 10 per cent men submitting to vasctomy, thus accounting for a total of 47 per cent family planning acceptors) tend to prefer a permanent method of averting future births to the temporary ones, having been persuaded by family planning campaigners to come to this irreversible decision after they had achieved the small family norm which, in their case, lay between one child and 3 children.

The lesser proportion of 17.3 per cent slum women (7.7 per cent using oral pills and 9.6 per cent accepting Copper T, both free of cost) have adopted these temporary devices, probably to space children under advice given to them by others. The extent of male domination in slum families is evidenced by the fact that, out of 193 or 64.3 per cent family planning acceptors, the proportion of women was the largest (139 or 46.3 per cent), which suggests that more men tend to put their women under birth control restrictions, and that it is only a few men (54 or 18 per cent in the sample) who, sparing their women, take the entire burden of family planning upon themselves.

Regular/irregular use of contraceptives

The sample reveals that, out of 300 slum families, the proportion of non-acceptors equalled 35.7 per cent, while those of the sterilised totalled 47.0 per cent. This leaves us with 17.3 per cent women contraceptive-users (7.7 per cent of those taking oral pills plus 9.6 per cent of those with Copper T insertions). Among these, 13.3 per cent were using contraceptives regularly, while the marginal proportion of 4 per cent used their contraceptives irregularly. The irregular use of temporary contraceptives may be attributed to their main purpose of spacing children. When they want to have a child, the women stop taking pills or get the Copper T taken out. Some slum women also said that on some day they forgot to take their daily pill.

Reasons for not favouring family planning

Out of the 300 slum families included in the survey, only 107 or 35.7 per cent were against family planning. Of these, the proportion of 29.3 per cent women frankly admitted that they knew nothing about the ins and outs of family planning. The smaller proportion of 5.7 per cent women confessed that once or twice when their husband resorted to withdrawal as a means of averting conception, or when he used a condom, both the partners did not enjoy sexual relation as they used to enjoy it before, and therefore both of them had returned to their former practice.

The almost negligible proportion of only 2 or 0.7 per cent slum wives were against family planning for different reasons.

One was of the opinion that 2 or 3 children were not enough for her, because she was not sure that everyone of them would survive. The other said that her children had grown big, and she wanted another baby of her own to play with as she used to do when her children were infants : to her, children about the age of four or five were sweeter than children above that age because older children were a constant headache to her for being willful and disobedient.

Desire for a child of the opposite sex

The majority of 64.3 per cent family planning acceptors informed the investigator that they had children of both sexes. Only a few had sons, and another few only daughters. They said that the number of children they had was enough, and it was immaterial for them if they happened to have no child of the opposite sex.

The non-acceptors of family planning were, however, divided over this issue. While 22.7 per cent of them seemed to unconsciously echo the message of SAARC which declared 1990 as the years of the girl child, the minority of 13 per cent insisted that, in their opinion, there must be at least a boy if their other children were all girls, and at least one girl if their other children were all boys, because brother-sister ties not only help the proper psychological growth of children but this relationship also proves useful in future years.

Impact of family planning on sex life

A few weeks after taking up either terminal or non-terminal measures, the largest proportion of 43 per cent respondents said that their sexual life remained unchanged. This gives the lie to the general belief prevailing among some ignorant men that vasectomy would affect their manhood adversely and also among orthodox women that tubectomy, being an offence against nature, nature will have its revenge.

Another sizeable proportion of 21.3 per cent women confessed that they felt better than before. Asked to elaborate further, they said that, being no longer afraid of an unwanted pregnancy, they enjoyed sex better than they did when they were in constant fear of conceiving against their will.

Signs of change after adopting family planning

While 12 per cent of the adopters of family planning complained of pain, the large proportion of 20.3 per cent confessed that there was no change in their condition : it was the same as before. The truth of the matter is that these women who had Copper T inserted admitted that they did feel somewhat uncomfortable during the first few days, but afterwards felt quite normal. There is also some pain after vasectomy when the effect of the local anaesthesia wears off, and there is also some pain in tubectomy when the woman wakes up from anaesthesia. As long as the incision is not fully healed up, the pain is bound to persist. Once the wound fills itself up and the stitches are removed, there should be no reason to feel any pain, unless something has gone wrong in the surgical operation.

Similarly, while no one complained that his or her health was reduced, 12.7 per cent slum respondents said that there was neither improvement nor deterioration in their health. The reason is not far to seek. Improvement in health may be due to the extinction of the fear psychosis arising from an unwanted pregnancy.

Family planning methods—easier for men or women ?

As compared to 29 per cent slum women who had undergone tubectomy, only 18 per cent men had submitted to vasectomy. This suggests that the slum men had not yet come to realise that sterilisation was easier for them, because (i) it takes less time, (ii) it is not a complicated procedure, (iii) it is less expensive for the Government, (iv) it enables man to return to work earlier, and (v) it does not affect virility at all.

Some men thought that sterilisation of women is easier after the delivery of the last of the required number of children, because the mother is still at the hospital and her physiological condition is most appropriate for tubectomy. The argument is true, but it betrays the selfishness of the male who still wants to retain his reproductive capacity for reasons deeply hidden in his heart.

As regards temporary methods of family planning, there was near unanimity that they were good only for the purpose of spacing children, and not for bringing about the final termination of births. The proportion of those who regarded temporary methods easier for women was the least in the sample—only 17.3 per cent. A few respondents reported that a double safety measure lay in the adoption of Nirodh by the husband as well as the regular intake of the pill by the wife.

Personal reaction to adoption of family planning methods

A small proportion of 6 per cent family planning adopters in the slum areas of urban Hoshangabad felt quite normal. They complained neither of loss of virility nor of diminution of pleasure. They were not self-conscious of any truncation of their manhood or of any split in their personality.

The smallest proportion of only 5 per cent slum men and women, after they recovered from sterilisation, felt a sense of pride in overcoming obstacles and objections, in having successfully carried out what they regarded as a personal and family necessity, in feeling liberated from the future bondage of child-bearing and child-rearing.

The highest proportion of 34 per cent adopters of family planning felt quite embarrassed at what they were doing, at least in the initial stages. They were sometimes nervous in the beginning, always conscious that the Copper T or the Mala pill was there. Those who had offered themselves for sterilisation were also nervous and somewhat afraid at the outset, but after some time it was smooth sailing for them.

Another proportion of 19.3 per cent from among the 47 sterilised men and women in the slums experienced a feeling of regret that they would have no more babies and what would happen if those they had were to die.

Reaction of elders

Only 21.3 per cent elders reacted favourably to the fertility control measures adopted by their married children, while the majority of 43 per cent reacted against what they termed "unnatural devices". Among those whose reactions were favourable, the writer knows a few elders who had 5 or more children, admitting they are happy that their married children favour a restricted family.

Some obstructionist elders are not content to register their protest verbally. When, in the teeth of their opposition, a young married member of their family, particularly their married daughter, undergoes family planning surgery, they make no attempt to conceal their displeasure and distaste for the son-in-law who induced his wife to opt for sterilisation. As it is, conversation with the interviewees revealed, that, in many cases, the parents of the girl secretly wished that the son-in-law should undergo surgery, while the parents of the boy wished in their heart of hearts that it is the daughter-in-law who should have offered herself for sterilisation.

Hesitation in admitting practising family planning

The majority of 39.6 per cent practitioners of planned parenthood feel no hesitation when they are asked whether they practise family planning because, in their opinion, no purpose is served in hiding what happens to be a fact, and not a taboo, what is not only legal but is also widely promoted by family planning programmers. It is only the minority of 24.7 respondents, largely the slum women, who hesitate to give a candid answer, especially to outsiders, to remote relatives, and to distant visitors with whom they are not on close terms.

Decision-makers of the size of the family

In the largest number 61.6 per cent cases, it were the family planning canvassers who had persuaded the slum families to take recourse to planned parenthood to limit the size of their family. The small proportion of only 2 per cent slum families reported that they had come round to the practice of family planning on the persuasive advice tendered by some other members of the family. It is only a fractional minority of only 0.7 respondents, all of them mothers of several children, who took the decision to halt the size of the family only after it was becoming quite unmanageable for them. The broad conclusion emerging from these responses is that the slum residents, although they may have been awakened to the consciousness of the merits of a small family, yet lack the initiative to come forward to adopt family planning measures : they still need the goading of others.

Feeling free after using a family planning method

We find that a proportion of 19.3 per cent slum couples, many of whom sterilised, did not feel any sense of liberation from the thraldom of child births and child-rearing. Haunted by doubts regarding the survival of their offspring/offsprings, they were most anxious when their child fell ill. An indirect benefit of this illness was that they gave the child the best medical treatment within their limited means and also the most careful nursing at home, heaving a sigh of relief when the child retrieved its health.

But the largest proportion of 45 per cent adopters of family planning methods, after having overcome their initial embarrassment or nervousness, enjoyed the feeling of freedom that goes with the regular use of a family planning method This was evident from their faces, their conversation, and their behaviour which was no longer darkened by clouds of fear.

Can more incentives by Government boost the family planning programme ?

The overwhelming majority of 63 per cent slum residents are in favour of incentives. This is understandable in the context of their generally lower economic status, the prevalence of illiteracy, and their poor living conditions. If the saying "money makes the mare go" is to be believed, it must be acted upon, and the amount of incentives—in cash or in kind—must be such as to generate a feeling among the residents that the rewards are worth going in for.

Only a negligible minority of 1.3 per cent slum families reported that they needed no incentives, because they were aware of the need for family planning against the backdrop of their own socio-economic constraints. While agreeing with their right thinking, one cannot but point out that the proportion of such people that think on the right lines is shockingly low—only 1.3 per cent. This calls for greater effort on the part of family planning educators to step up their campaign to raise the proportion of 1.3 per cent to a much higher level, which would be a more convincing testimony to the success of the family planning programme than the mere fulfilment of annual targets.

Should Government impose a fine on the birth of the third and subsequent child ?

The majority of 63.6 per cent slum residents prefer the democratic method of voluntary family planning. They therefore reject the idea that Government should impose a fine on the birth of the third and subsequent child. The fractional minority of 0.7 per cent slum respondents favour the imposition of fine on those couples who beget a third child or more. These hardliners are impatient of the tardy process of democratic motivation and want quicker results by favouring compulsory family planning after the second child.

Additional incentives for boosting sterilisation

The top rank (52.0 per cent) goes to those slum families adopting family planning measures who believe that liberal loans from banks for business and agricultural activities will go a long way in bringing a larger number of individuals to the operation table. These persons obviously represent those who feel difficulty in obtaining loans from banks with personal efforts and/or those to whom the sum loaned is insufficient for the kind of business/ agricultural operations they envisage.

The second place (7.7 per cent) is occupied by those family planning acceptors who hold the view that priority in allotment of residential plots and Government housing would be a sufficient inducement to help the needy slum families to volunteer themselves for vasectomy and tubectomy. Some of these persons were low-paid servants of the Central and State Government or semi-Government organisations who had not been allotted Government accommodation till the time the survey was undertaken.

The bottom place (4.6 per cent) is relegated to those slum residents who feel that time-scale promotions will attract other employees to the terminal methods of family planning. Apparently, these interviews are also Government/semi-Government employees who, impatient of having to wait for the long time it takes promotion to fall due in the ordinary course of time, long for time-bound promotions to enjoy higher pay and pay-scale till their superannuation.

Taken together, all the three additional incentives may be taken up on an experimental basis for a couple of years, since they are not only manageable but also do not impose any great burden on the exchequer; and, if the results are encouraging, these measures may be continued, otherwise they may be reviewed or totally withdrawn.

Choice of methods to attract more people to family planning

The majority of 63.0 per cent slum families are in favour of incentives coupled with social work. The slum families are largely illiterate or quasi-literate and slow to react to non-traditional ideas. Hence constant dinning into their ears what they should do, supported by irrefutable proof of the favourable results achieved by those who have already adopted family planning, would bring conviction among them regarding the merits of planned parenthood.

The almost negligible minority of 1.3 per cent of hardcore slum residents insist that, unless stringent measures are imposed, it will take several decades to achieve the optimum level of population growth.

Can family size be planned ?

The substantial majority of 63.0 per cent slum families in urban Hoshangabad in the sample survey have a positive attitude towards the limitation of the family size. Among the non-acceptors of family planning, some slum families reported that they were not sure they could plan their family. A few women had reservations whether they would be permitted by their husbands or in-laws to do so. The orthodox among the slum residents still clung to the "children are a gift of God" theory.

Any objection if children adopt family planning methods after marriage ?

According to Table 51, 63.0 per cent slum families believed that the size of the family could be and should be planned. In Table 53, the percentage of those who would like their married children to take up family planning rises to 67.3, showing an increase of 3.0 per cent.

These statistical figures suggest that, among the non-acceptors, a small proportion of 3.0 per cent have come to feel that, while they do not favour family planning in their own case, they would raise no objection if their children, after marriage, adopted family planning measures. This reduces the percentage of hardliners from 35.7 to 32.7. Who knows that, with the effluxion of time, there might be a further change for the better in their attitude as well as in the attitude of their children when they marry.

Initiative in family planning

The sample reveals that 193 or 64.3 per cent slum families, who had adopted family planning did not do so on their own : they were motivated by others, mostly by official family planning programmers, thus showing clearly the lack of initiative. Now that they had been initiated into family planning and had come to know what it was all about, they reported that they were prepared to take the lead.

Those using non-terminal methods are now fully prepared to take the first step (i) in changing their present non-terminal method to some other non-terminal method as and when it suits their convenience, or (ii) in switching over from a temporary method to a permanent method as and when necessity arises. The 107 or 35.7 per cent non-acceptors, still clinging to the obscurantism of their traditions, evidently lack initiative.

Education regarding family planning and its adoption

The sample reveals that 35.7 per cent of the slum families were adamant in not accepting family planning, in spite of all efforts on the part of family planning campaigners and others to persuade them to adopt it. But the majority of 64.3 per cent slum families reported that adequate education was being imparted to people on family planning and its adoption, the evidence of which was that, influenced by that education, they were now planning their families.

All these responses show that, in planning a family, the slum people put their family interest first and foremost, which is by no means wrong. After all, the norm of planned families is a part of the larger goal of national development programmes : the success of one is dependent on the success of the other.

Responsibility of parents in helping their children to develop a favourable attitude towards a small family

A handful of slightly educated slum residents argued that education, aiming at the inculcation of a favourable attitude towards a small family, must be imparted, scientifically and in a simple language, in the higher classes in schools as well as in undergraduate courses in colleges and universities in combination with a suitable allied subject, whatever its nomenclature, because even if some parents are knowledgeable they do not possess costly models and charts essential for this purpose.

A few respondents had a point when they suggested that 2-week, 3-week, or 4-week condensed courses should be conducted free twice a year in State hospitals, dispensaries, health centres, and even private maternity and nursing homes for the benefit of young people during summer vacations, winter vacations, or Dussehra-Diwali vacations, with the option of attending any one of them according to their convenience.

Polygamy and its purpose

The main reason for adopting polygamy, as reported by the majority of 67.0 per cent slum residents, is the quenching of sexual thirst. Where the husband comes home too tired or drunk and goes to sleep, or has been away from home for many months, or has been ill for a long time, or is partly or wholly impotent, and the wife feels unsatisfied and somebody to her liking is easily available, illicit polygamy seems to be the only way out.

A sizeable number of 31.7 per cent respondents affirmed that cohabitation with the same person in the same manner leads to monotony which can be dispelled by variety and novelty with another person.

The small minority of only 1.3 per cent slum respondents generously maintained that if a woman desirous of achieving motherhood and disappointed of ever having a child from her lawful husband, tends to gratify her maternal instinct by mating with another man, with or without the consent and connivance of her lawful husband, in order to conceive a child who, when delivered, passes off for all practical purposes as the legitimate child of the married couple, they would turn a blind eye on it.

There seems to be a good deal of truth in what the slum respondents reported, but the investigator did not come across specific cases of polygamy in the slum areas surveyed by her. What was said by the respondents was, more less hypothetical, and could not be corroborated by concrete evidence.

Should the system of polygamy be changed ?

While denying the prevalence of polygamy in their residential areas, the majority of 99.3 per cent slum respondents reported that wherever the system of polygamy prevailed. it must be changed, because the very idea of a woman having more than one husband was revolting to them.

The fractional minority of only 0.7 per cent slum respondents said that, while they were against the system of polygamy, they would not like to deny a woman the fulfilment of her motherhood when the fault lay not in herself but in her husband, and divorce under their circumstances was neither desirable nor possible. In such a case, if the woman has the child with another man in a hush-hush manner, and both husband and wife and happy with the child, they would not raise their eyebrows in protest.

Favouring widow remarriage

The largest majority of 99 per cent slum families favour widow remarriage, irrespective of whether the widow in young or not, self-supporting or dependent, issueless or with children. A negligible minority of only one per cent respondents were hostile to widow remarriage. They said they had been told that remarriage of widows had been banned for several centuries, and that some men imbued with new fangled ideas advocated widow remarriage. They further said that a widow was an inauspicious being, who brings bad luck to people, and for this reason she is deprived to many good things of life.

Should parents explain the facts of life to their children ?

The majority of 67.3 per cent respondents were of the view that facts of life must be explained to their children, but the obligation to do so must fall less on parents and more on educational institutions, voluntary organisations, specially on family planning programmers who should conduct short-duration courses, in the context of the prevailing socio-economic scenario, for boys and girls emerging out of their adolescence.

Conclusion

In the light of the above findings, the main hypothesis of the study—the common belief about the slum residents breeding fast and resisting social change in the context of family planning programmes as operating at present is no longer tenable—has proved true.

The related hypothetical propositions, determining whether he hypothesis is true or not, have also been verified. Thus,

(i) there is interlinkage between the level of education and the extent of planned parenthood;

(ii) the total monthly income of a family is one among the several factors contributing to family welfare;

(iii) the age-difference between the spouses is immaterial when couples adopt family planning methods, irrespective of the fact whether they were motivated by others or were self-motivated;

(iv) surgical methods are preferred by couples who have more than the desired number of children, while other acceptors of family planning tend to adopt mechanical methods for spacing children;

(v) sterilisation affects neither a man's virility nor a woman's sex life, and the temporary methods of fertility control also do not cause discomfort in the long run;

(vi) the initial reaction to the adoption of a family planning method is generally of embarrassment or apprehension which gradually disappears;

(vii) some elders in the slums have begun to realise that they would raise no objection if their married children take up family planning;

(viii) the slum couples arrive at the decision to limit their families after a good deal of persuasion; and

(ix) the slum families undergo sterilisation to halt future births once and for all, the incentives serving as compensation for working time/days lost.

In other words, there is considerable evidence of social change in terms of the family planning programme in the slum areas of urban Hoshangabad.

BIBLIOGRAPHY

Adams, B.N., *TheFamily : A Sociological Interpretation.* Rand McNally, Chicago, 1976.

Agarwal, S.N., and D.S. Arora, *Women in Rural Society,* Vohra Publishers, Allahabad, 1989.

Agarwal, S.N., *India's Population Problems,* Tata-McGraw, New Delhi, 1984.

Ali, Ameer, *The Spirit of Islam,* Ashraf Brothers, reprint, Lahore, 1984.

Allport, G.W., *The Nature of Prejudice,* Addison-Wesley Publishing Co., Reading, Massachussetts, 1964.

Altekar, A.S., *The Position of Women in Hindu Civilisation,* Motilal Banarsi Das, Varanasi, 1962.

Anderson, M., ed., *Sociology of the Family,* 2nd ed., Penguin, New York, 1980.

Baghel, D.S., *Nagriya Samaj Shastra* (Urban Sociology), M.P. Granth Academy, Bhopal, 1986 (Hindi).

Bannerji, D., *Family Planning in India : A Critique and Perspective,* Vikas Publishing House, New Delhi, 1981.

Bem, D., Beliefs, *Attitudes and Human Affairs,* Brooks—Col, Belmont, California, 1970.

Benedict, R., *Patterns of Culture,* Houghton Mifflin, Boston, 1969.

Bernard, Jessie, *Remarriage,* Dryden, New York, 1966.

Bernard, Jessie, *The Future of Marriage,* World Books, New York, 1982.

Berscheid, Ellen, and E.H. Walster, *Interpersonal Attraction,* Addison-Wesley, Reading, Massachussetts, 1979.

Bhushan, Vidya, *Sociology,* Kitab Mahal, Allahabad, 1979.

Blood, Robert, P., *Marriage,* Collier-Macmillan, London, 1969.

Blood, R.O. Jr. and D.M. Wolfe, *Husbands and Wives,* Free Press, New York, 1970.

Bogardus, E.S., *Sociology,* Macmillan, New York, 1970.

Bowlby, J.A., *Attachment and Loss,* Basic Books, New York, 1969.

Bowman, H.A., *Marriage for Moderns,* McGraw Hill, New York, 1964.

Burgess, E.W. and H.J. Locke, *The Family : From Institution to Companionship,* American Book Co., New York, 1965.

Burgess, E.W. and H.J. Locke, *The Family*, American Book Co., New York, 1970.

Burgess, E.W., and H.J. Locke, *Engagement and Marriage*, Lippincott, Philedelphia, 1973.

Campbell, J.K., *Honour, Family, and Patronage*, Clarendon Press, Oxford, 1974.

Centers, R., *The Psychology of Social Classes*, Princeton University Press, Princeton, New Jersey, 1969.

Charthau, R., *Sex Manners for Young Generation*, New English Library, London, 1980.

Chauhan, Indira, *Purdah to Profession*, B.R. Publishing Corporation, Delhi, 1985.

Chesser, E., *Cost of Loving*, Methuen, London, 1974.

Chesser, E., *Twentieth Century Women*, Arrow Books Ltd., London, 1979.

Chibbar, Y.P., *From Caste to Class*, Associated Publishing House, New Delhi, 1968.

Cristensen, H.A., ed., *Handbook of Family and Marriage*, Rand McNally, Chicago, 1984.

Cormick, Margaret, *She Who Rides a Peacock : Indian-Students and Social Change*, Asia Publishing House, Bombay, 1961.

Davidson, K., R.B. Ginsberg, and H.H. Kay, *Sex-based Discrimination*, St. Paul, Minnesota, 1974.

Davis, Maximi, *The Sexual Responsibility of Women*, Perona Books, New York, 1970.

Davis, Kingsley, *Human Society,* Macmillan, New York, 1973.

D'Souza, Anthony, *The Indian Family in Change,* Sterling Publishers, New Delhi, 1973.

D'Souza, Anthony, *Happiness in Marriage,* Indian Social Institute, New Delhi, 1975.

Dube, Pushpashri, *Jan Sankhya Shikshan* (Population Education), Vivek Prakashan, New Delhi, 1983 (Hindi).

Duberman, L., *The Reconstituted Family,* Nelson Hall, Chicago, 1975.

Duvall, E.M., and R. Hill, *Being Married,* Association Press, New York, 1970.

Ehrmann, W., Premarital *Sexual Behaviour,* Bantam Books, New York, 1970.

Ellis, Havelock, *Sex and Marriage,* Pyramid Books, New York, 1961.

Epstein, Cynthia, F., *Woman's Place,* University of California Press, Berkeley, 1980.

Fairchild, H.P., *Dictionary of Sociology and Related Sciences,* Littlefield—Adams, Paterson, New Jersey, 1974.

Federic, Ronald, *Sociology,* Addison-Wesley Publishing Co., Reading, Massachussetts, 1975.

Fieldman, K.A., and T.M. Newcomb, *The Impact of College on Students,* Vol. I, Jossey-Bass, San Francisco, 1979.

Fonesca, Mabel, *Counselling for Marital Happiness,* Manaktala, Bombay, 1966.

Foster, G.M. *Traditional Societies and Technological Change,* Harper and Row, New York, 1982.

Gavanagh, W., *Marriage Counselling,* American Press Ltd., New York, 1978.

Ghurye, G.S., *Caste and Class in India,* Popular Book Depot, Bombay, 1950.

Ghurye, G.S., *Caste, Class and Occupation,* Popular Prakashan, Bombay, 1961.

Goode, W.J., *World Revolution and Family Patterns,* Free Press, New York, 1973.

Goode, W.J., *The Family,* Prentice-Hall of India, New Delhi, 1975.

Goode, W.J., *Principles of Sociology,* Tata McGraw-Hill, New Delhi, 1979.

Gore, M.S., *Urbanisation and Family Change,* Popular Prakashan, Bombay, 1966.

Gross, I.H., E.W. Crandell, and M.M. Knoll, *Management for Modern Families,* 4th ed., Prentice-Hall, Englewood Cliffs, New Jersey, 1980.

Gupta, M., *Gramin Samaj Shastra : Bharat Parivesh Mein,* (Rural Sociology of India), Vivek Prakashan, New Delhi, 1985 (Hindi).

Hate, Chandrakala, *Changing Status of Women,* Allied Publishers, New Delhi, 1969.

Havemann, E., *Birth Control,* Time-Life Books, 1977.

Havemann, E., and M. Lehtinen, *Marriages and Families,* Prentice-Hall, Englewood Cliffs, New Jersey, 1986.

Howe, L.K., ed., *The Future of the Family*, Simon and Schuster, New York, 1972.

Hutton, J.H., *Caste in India*, Oxford University Press, Bombay, 1961.

Kandel, D.B., and G.S. Lesser, *Youth in Two Worlds*, Jossey-Bass, New York, 1982.

Kannan, C.T., *Inter-caste and Inter-community marriage in India*, Allied Publishers, Bombay, 1963.

Kapadia, K.M., *Marriage and Family in India*, Oxford University Press, Bombay, 8th impression, 1984.

Kapur, Promilla, *Love, Marriage and Sex*, Vikas Publishing House, New Delhi, 1973.

Kinsey, A.C., W.B. Pomeroy, and C.E. Martin, *Sexual Behaviour in the Human Male*, Saunders, Philedelphia, 1948.

Kinsey, A.C., *Sexual Behaviour in the Human Female*, Saunders, Philedelphia, 1953.

Kirkpatrick, C., *The Family as Process and Institution*, Ronald, New York, 2nd ed., 1963.

Klausner, S., ed., *The Quest for Self-Control*, Free Press of Glencoe, New York, 1979.

Kogan, B.A., *Human Sexual Expression*, Harcourt Bruce, new York, 1973.

Kohn, M.L., *Class and Conformity*, Dorsey, Homewood, Illinois, 1979.

Kuppuswamy, B., *Social Change in India*, Vikas Publishing House, Delhi, 1982.

Lanty, H.R., and E.C. Snyder, *Marriage : An Examination of Man-Woman Relationship,* John Wiley and Sons, New York, 1979.

Lundberg, G.A., *Foundations of Sociology,* Macmillan, New York, 1966.

Laumann, E.O., P.M. Siegal, and R.W. Hodge, *The Logic of Social Hierarcy,* Markham Press, Chicago, 1970.

Leaba, C., *The Sexual Nature of Man,* Doubleday, Emden City, New York, 1964.

Levy, J., and R. Munroe, *The Happy Family,* Knopfs, New York, 1969.

Lindsey, B.B., and W. Evans, *The Companionate Marriage,* Boni and Liveright, New York, 1927.

Lopata, H.Z., *Occupation : Housewife,* Oxford University Press, New York, 1972.

Maccoby, E.E., and C.N. Jacklin, *The Psychology of Sex Differences,* Stanford University Press, Stanford, California, 1974.

Mace, D.R., and V.C. Mace, *We Can Have Better Marriages,* Abingdon, Press, New York, 1974.

Majumdar, D.N., and T.N. Madan, *Introduction to Social Anthropology,* Asia Publishing House, Bombay, Rpt., 1977.

Malinowsky, P., *Sex Repression in Savage Society,* Kegan Paul, London, 1977.

Mamoria, C.B., *Population and Family Planning,* Asia Publishing House, Bombay, 1970.

Mamoria, C.B., *Social Problems and Social Disorganisation,* Kitab Mahal, Allahabad, 7th ed., 1980.

Masters, W.H., and V.E. Johnson, *Human Sexual Response,* Little, Brown, Boston, 1966.

Masters, W.H., V.E. Johnson, *Human Sexual Inadequacy,* Little, Brown, Boston, 1970.

Masters, W.H., and V.E. Johnson, *The Pleasure Bond,* Bantam Books, New York, 1976.

Maurya, S.B., *Women in India,* Chugh Publications, Allahabad, 1988.

Mazur, R., *The New Intimacy,* Beacon Press, Boston, 1973.

McCall, George, ed., *Social Relations,* Aldine, Chicago, 1980.

Mead, Margaret, *Male and Female,* Doubleday Morrow Co., New York, 1977.

Mehta, Rama, *The Western Educated Hindu Women,* Asia Publishing House, Bombay, 1970.

Merchant, K.T., *Changing Views on Marriage and the Family,* B.G. Paul and Co., Madras, 1965.

Misra, B.B., *The Indian Middle Class,* Oxford University Press, London, 1971.

Money, J., and Ehrhardt, *Man and Woman, Boy and Girl,* John Hopkins, Baltimore, 1982.

Montagu, Ashley, *The Natural Superiority of Women,* Collier, rev. ed., New York, 1980.

Moore, W.E., *Social Change,* Prentice-Hall, Englewood Cliffs, New Jersey, 1973.

Mukherjee, Prabhati, *Hindu Women*, Orient Longman, New Delhi, 1970.

Mumford, Lewis, *The Culture of Cities*, Harcourt Brace, New York, 1970.

Myrdal, A., and V. Klein, *Women's Two Roles : Home and Work*, Routledge, London, 1956.

Nath, Surendra, *Santati Nirodh* (Heredity Transmission), M.P. Hindi Granth Academy, Bhopal, 1987 (Hindi).

Nye, F.I., and F.M. Berardo, *The Family*, Macmillan, New York, 1983.

Ogburn, W.F., and M.E. Nimkoff, *A Handbook of Sociology*, Routledge and Keagan Paul, London, 1960.

O'Neill, N., *The Marriage Process*, M. Evans and Co., New York, 1977.

Pillai, S.P., *Birth Control Simplified*, Allied Publishers, New Delhi, 1984.

Pomerai, R.D., *The Future of Sex Relationships*, Keagan Paul, London, 1967.

Prabha, Pandhari, *Hindu Social Organisation*, Popular Book Depot, Bombay, 1964.

Presthus, R., *The Organisational Society*, Vintage Books, New York, 1972.

Raina, K.B.L., *Family Planning*, D.K. Publishers, New Delhi, 1982.

Radhakrishnan, S., *Religion and Society*, Allen and Unwin, London, 1959.

Rampal, S.N., *Indian Women and Sex*, Printox, New Delhi, 1978.

Rokeach, M., *The Open and Closed Mind*, Basic Books, New York, 1970.

Rapoport, R., and R.D. Rapoport, *Families*, Penguin Books, Baltimore, 1974.

Rapoport, R. and R.D. Rapoport, *Leisure and Family Life Cycle*, Routledge and Kegan Paul, London, 1975.

Rosenbaum, S., and I. Algers, eds., *The Marriage Relationship : Psychoanalytic Perspective*, Basic Books, New York, 1980.

Roy, D., and R. Roy, *Honest Sex*, American Library, New York, 1978.

Russell, Bertrand, *Marriage and Morals*, Bantam Books, New York, 1977.

Safilos-Rothschild, C., *Love, Sex, and Sex Roles*, Prentice-Hall, Englewood Cliffs, New Jersey, 1977.

Satyavati, D.K., *Family Planning and Birth Control*, National Books, Bombay, 1982.

Segal, J., and Z. Segal, *Growing Up Smart and Happy*, McGraw Hill, New York, 1984.

Sennet, R., and J. Cobb, *The Hidden Injuries of Class*, Vintage Books, New York, 1973.

Schlesinger, B., *The One Parent Family*, University of Toronto Press, Toronto, 1980.

Sharma, L.N., *Saral Parivar Niyojan* (Easy Family Planning), Rajpal and Sons, New Delhi, 1986 (Hindi).

Sharma, L.N., *Pati Patni* (Husband and Wife), Rajpal and Sons, New Delhi, 1986 (Hindi).

Sharma, L.N., *Birth Control*, Rajpal and Sons, New Delhi, 1987.

Shuck, M., S. Tangri, and L.W. Hoffman, eds., *Women and Achievement*, Halstead, New York, 1975.

Silverberg, K., *Prestige, Class, and Mobility*, Gyldendel, Copenhagen, 1969.

Singh, K., *Principles of Sociology*, Prakash Kendra, Lucknow, 1985.

Singh, S.D., *Parivar aur Samaj* (Family and Society), Kamal Prakashan, Indore, 1986 (Hindi).

Skolnick, A., *The Intimate Environment*, Little, Brown, Boston, 1973.

Skolnick, A., and J.H. Skolnick, *Intimacy, Family, and Society*, Little, Brown, Boston, 1974.

Smith, J.R. and L.J. Smith, *Beyond Marriage*, John Hopkins University Press, Baltimore, 1974.

Srinivas, M.N., *Social Change in Modern India*, University of California Press, Berkeley, 1966.

Srinivas, M.N., *Caste in Modern India*, Asia Publishing House, Bombay, 1964.

Starr, B.D., and M.B. Weiner, *Sex and Sexuality in Mature Years*, Stein and Day, New York, 1981.

Steinmetz, S., A.S. Murray, *Violence in Family*, Dodd Mead, New York, 1974.

Stephens, W.N., *The Family in Cross Cultural Perspective*, Holt, Rinehart and Winston, New York, 1973.

Tomar, R.B.S., and Others, *Gramin Samaj Shastra*, (Rural Sociology), Sri Ram Mehra and Co., Agra, 1983 (Hindi).

Tomar, R.B.S., and Others, *Parivar aur Samaj*, Sri Ram Mehra and Co., Agra, 1985 (Hindi).

Walker, K., *Marriage and Family in a Changing World*, London, 1975.

Weiss, R.L., *Marital Separation*, G. and C. Merriam, Springfield, Illinois, 1973.

Westermarck, Edward, *History of Human Marriage*, Macmillan, London, 1925.

Westermarck, Edward, *The Future of Marriage*, Events Publishing Co., New York, 1928.

Williams, R.J., *Biochemical Individuality*, Wiley, New York, 1976.

Winch, R.F., *Male Selection*, Harper and Brothers, New York, 1978.

Winch, R.F., *The Modern Family*, Holt, 5th ed., 1981.

Young, M., and P. Willmolt, *The Symmetrical Family*, Pantheon, New York, 1974.

Zablocki, B.D., *The Joyful Community*, Penguin Books, Baltimore 1981.

Zawacki, A.A., *A Textbook for Family Planning Workers*, University of Chicago, Chicago, 1981.

Zigler, E., and I.R. Child, *Socialisation and Personality Development*, Addison-Wesley, Reading, Massachussetts, 1973.

REPORTS

Census Reports of 1951, 1961, 1971, and 1981, Publications Division, Ministry of Information and Broadcasting, New Delhi.

India 1986, Publications Division, Ministry of Information and Broadcasting, New Delhi, 1987.

National Family Welfare Programme in Madhya Pradesh, Health and Family Welfare Department, Bhopal, 1988.

National Population Policy, Publications Division, Ministry of Information and Broadcasting, New Delhi, 1986.

World Population and Resources : Report by Political and Economic Planning Bureau, Morello and Co., London, 1979.

QUESTIONNAIRE

PERSONAL DATA :

1. Sex : Male/Female
2. Age :
3. Address :
4. Marital Status
   - (a) Married :
   - (b) Unmarried :
   - (c) Widow :
   - (d) Divorced :
   - (e) Separated :
5. Level of Education
   - (a) Illiterate :
   - (b) Literate :
   - (c) Primary :
   - (d) Middle School :
   - (e) Secondary :
   - (f) 10 + 2 :

6. Occupation
   (a) Employment :
   (b) Business :
   (c) Agriculture :

FAMILY DATA

1. Total No. of Family Members :
2. (a) No. of Siblings :
   Brothers :
   Sisters :
   Parent-in-law :
   Sisters and Brothers-in-law :
3. Education
   Father's :
   Mother's :
   Husband's/Wife's :

ECONOMIC STATUS OF FAMILY (TOTAL INCOME) :

1. (a) Unemployed :
   (b) Below Rs. 1,000 :
   (c) Rs. 1,001 to 1,500 :
   (d) Rs. 1,501 to 2,000 :
   (e) Rs. 2,001 to 2,500 :
   (f) Above Rs. 2,500 :
2. Do you save money : Yes/No
   If not why ? :
   If Yes :
   (a) In Bank :
   (b) Post Office :
   (c) Investment in business :
   (d) Any other :

DATA ON FAMILY PLANNING :

1. Are you in favour of early marriage ? : Yes/No
2. At what age did you marry ? : Specify
   - (a) Below 18 years :
   - (b) Between 18 years and 20 years :
   - (c) Between 21 years and 25 years :
   - (d) Above 25 years :
3. What is the difference between the age of husband and wife ?
   - (a) Less than 3 years :
   - (b) 3 to 6 years :
   - (c) 6 to 9 years :
   - (d) Above 9 years :
   - (e) Both of equal age :
4. How many surviving children do you have ?

Age	*Boys*	*Girls*

5. Where your children were born ?
   - (a) Government Hospital :
   - (b) Private maternity/nursing home :
   - (c) At own home :
   - (d) At father/Mother-in-law's :

6. How old were you when your first child was born ?
   - (a) Below 18 years :
   - (b) 18-20 years :
   - (c) 21-25 years :
   - (d) 26-30 years :
7. When was the youngest Born ?
   - (a) 18-20 years :
   - (b) 21-25 years :
   - (c) 26-30 years :
   - (d) 31-35 years :
   - (e) Over 35 years :
8. Do you want more children ? : Yes/No
9. Are you in favour of family planning ? If not, why ?

   If yes, which method do you prefer ?

   (number them according to preference).
   - (a) Natural methods :
     - (i) Celibacy (Brahmacharya) :
     - (ii) Late marriage :
     - (iii) Moral restraint :
   - (b) Biological Methods :
     - (i) Coitus Interruptus :
     - (ii) Rhythm method :
   - (c) Chemical Methods :
     - (i) Foam tablets :
     - (ii) Jelley :
     - (iii) Oral pills :
   - (d) Mechanical methods :
     - (i) Diaphrams :

(ii) Condom :

(iii) Intra-Uterine Device :

(e) Surgical Methods

(i) Sterilisation

Vasectomy (male operation) :

Tubectomy (female operation):

(ii) Medical termination of pregnancy :

10. Do you use them regularly ? : Yes/No

11. If you are not in favour of family planning, is it because ;

(a) You have not enough information about family planning :

(b) You do not enjoy sexual life :

(c) Two or three children are not enough :

12. If a family has two or three children of the same sex, should they try to get one more child of opposite sex ? : Yes/No

13. Does Your adoption of family planning affect your sexual life : : Yes/No

If yes, is it

(a) Better than before

(b) Worse than before :

(c) Unchanged :

14. Do you feel any change or sign or physical discomfort or change after your adoption of family planning ?

	Increased	*Reduced*	*Same*
(a) Any pain			
(b) Condition of health			

(c) Any other ? Specify

15. Do you think that adoption of a method of family planning by male is easier than that by a female ?
    (a) Permanent methods : Yes/No
    (b) Temporary methods : Yes/No
16. What is your reaction when anybody asks you about the fact that you adopt family planning method ?
    (a) Embarrassed :
    (b) Sad :
    (c) Proud :
    (d) Normal :
17. What was your elder's attitude regarding it ?
    (a) Favourable :
    (b) Unfavourable :
18. Do you have any hesitation in saying clearly that you practise family planning ? : Yes/No
19. Who decides the size of your family ?
    (a) You yourself ;
    (b) Government :
    (c) Husband/Wife :
    (d) Other family members :
20. Do you feel more free after using a family planning method ? : Yes/No

INCENTIVES :

1. Can more incentives by Government boost the family planning programme : Yes/No
2. Should Government impose a fine on the birth of third and subsequent child ? : Yes/No

3. Should Government give the following incentives to boost family planning operations ?

S. No.	*Incentives*	*Yes*	*No*
(1)	Priority in the allotment of plots and houes		
(2)	Time-scale promotion for employees		
(3)	Liberal loans from banks for business		

4. By which of the following methods will more people be attracted to family planning.
   - (a) Incentives and social work :
   - (b) Restrictions :
   - (c) Any other :

1. Do you believe that family size can be planned ? : Yes/No
2. Do you have any objection if your children adopt family planning methods after marriage ? : Yes/No
3. Will you take the initiative in adopting family planning ? : Yes/No
4. Do you think people are being educated regarding family planning and its adoption ? : Yes/No
5. Do you think that parents have a responsibility to help their children fo develop a favourable attitude towards a small family ? : Yes/No
6. Polygamy is adopted
   - (a) To quench sexual thirst :

(b) For novelty :

(c) Having a child :

7. Do you feel this system must be changed ? : Yes/No

8. Are you in favour of widow re-marriage ? : Yes/No

9. Should the parents explain the facts of life to their children ? : Yes/No

INDEX